Knowing Me, Knowing You

The PEP Personality Process

NADINE HANCHAR

BALBOA
PRESS
A DIVISION OF HAY HOUSE

Copyright © 2018 Nadine Hanchar.

All rights reserved. No part of this book may be used or reproduced by any means, graphic, electronic, or mechanical, including photocopying, recording, taping or by any information storage retrieval system without the written permission of the author except in the case of brief quotations embodied in critical articles and reviews.

Balboa Press books may be ordered through booksellers or by contacting:

Balboa Press
A Division of Hay House
1663 Liberty Drive
Bloomington, IN 47403
www.balboapress.com
1 (877) 407-4847

Because of the dynamic nature of the Internet, any web addresses or links contained in this book may have changed since publication and may no longer be valid. The views expressed in this work are solely those of the author and do not necessarily reflect the views of the publisher, and the publisher hereby disclaims any responsibility for them.

The author of this book does not dispense medical advice or prescribe the use of any technique as a form of treatment for physical, emotional, or medical problems without the advice of a physician, either directly or indirectly. The intent of the author is only to offer information of a general nature to help you in your quest for emotional and spiritual well-being. In the event you use any of the information in this book for yourself, which is your constitutional right, the author and the publisher assume no responsibility for your actions.

Any people depicted in stock imagery provided by Getty Images are models, and such images are being used for illustrative purposes only.
Certain stock imagery © Getty Images.

Print information available on the last page.

ISBN: 978-1-9822-1305-3 (sc)
ISBN: 978-1-9822-1304-6 (hc)
ISBN: 978-1-9822-1306-0 (e)

Library of Congress Control Number: 2018911413

Balboa Press rev. date: 01/03/2019

Dedicated to my father, James "Jim" Patrick Robertson, 1918–2007. Below is the poem I wrote for his celebration of life, where we planted a hawthorn tree in his honour in the park he helped to create.

I Dedicate This Hawthorn Tree...

I dedicate this hawthorn tree
Because of all the lessons my daddy taught to me.
When I was very, very small,
He taught me pure love was unconditional.

As I grew and grew some more,
He taught me work really didn't have to be a chore,
That it was okay to love what you do,
To be dedicated and fully responsible too.

He taught me that silence and wisdom often went together;
To think things through, during emotional weather;
To make sure to have patience, kindness, and to give respect;
Through your honesty and loyalty, to truly connect;

That people and family had to come first,
And that continued learning could be your thirst;
To look out for your neighbour, your sister, your brother;
To use your intelligence and strength to help one another.

His actions often spoke louder than words,
And his dry sense of humour could have won him awards.
He made time for both the big and the small,
And his smile was infectious—yes, infectious to all.

As we both continued to grow much older,
I learned from him that I could be bolder,
That change could be a good thing too,
And making a difference was the right thing to do.

He taught me to listen to the voice of my heart,
For all of life's lessons it would surely impart.
He taught me to make the best of each moment—
That there's not enough time to be caught in the torrent.

So with honour and true integrity,
I dedicate this hawthorn tree,
Yes, I dedicate this hawthorn tree
Because of all the lessons, all the lessons
that my dad, he taught to me.

Acknowledgements

A special thank-you to my husband, Heinz, who has supported me through the ups and downs of getting this book published and who has loved me through the process.

Thank you to Miriam MacPhail, a friend of many years and a wonderful graphic designer who did the graphics for this book.

I would also like to thank the ladies in my Master Mind group, who were really instrumental in inspiring the project along.

I would like to thank my cheerleaders, Mary Kerr and Deb Eagleson-Pepper, who over the years never gave up on me.

I would like to thank my teachers, trainers, and mentors, who are many and who cover such a wide range of fields and topics.

I want to acknowledge Jen Violi, Neil Dickie, and M. Starr, who all contributed to the editing of this book.

Thanks to Lisa Vyas and Mary Oxley of Balboa Press, who saw me through the process of getting this book published.

From my heart, I want to acknowledge all of my clients, students, family members, and friends—from those who have touched my life briefly to those who are in my life still. I want to say that without you, this book would not have been possible.

I have had the privilege of knowing and working with so many magnificent people who have blessed my life in so many different ways, and I want you all to know how much I appreciate you! The impact of each individual has contributed greatly to who I am today, and I live in eternal gratitude.

Contents

Introduction xi

Part One: An Overview of the PEP Personality Process 1
    Chapter 1:   The PEP Personality Process 3
    Chapter 2:   How to Assess Your Processing Style 8
    Chapter 3:   How to Use This Book 14

Part Two: The Environmental Zone 19
    Chapter 4:   The Environmental Zone: Kinesthetic 21
    Chapter 5:   The Environmental Zone: Visual 24
    Chapter 6:   The Environmental Zone: Cognitive 26
    Chapter 7:   The Environmental Zone: Auditory 28

Part Three: The Communication Zone 31
    Chapter 8:   The Communication Zone: Kinesthetic 35
    Chapter 9:   The Communication Zone: Visual 51
    Chapter 10: The Communication Zone: Cognitive 68
    Chapter 11: The Communication Zone: Auditory 89
    Chapter 12: How to Quickly Identify the Different
                      Communication Styles 110

Part Four: The Challenge Zone 115
    Chapter 13: The Challenge Zone: Kinesthetic 117
    Chapter 14: The Challenge Zone: Visual 122
    Chapter 15: The Challenge Zone: Cognitive 128
    Chapter 16: The Challenge Zone: Auditory 133

Part Five: The Security Zone 139
    Chapter 17: The Security Zone: Kinesthetic 141
    Chapter 18: The Security Zone: Visual 143

Chapter 19: The Security Zone: Cognitive 146
Chapter 20: The Security Zone: Auditory 149

Part Six: Engaging and Bridging 153

Chapter 21: The PEP Personality Process in Relationships 155
Chapter 22: The PEP Personality Process in Teaching,
                    Facilitating, and Learning 170
Chapter 23: Utilizing the Processing Styles in Business 176
Chapter 24: Processing Styles in Selling and Marketing 187

Conclusion 191
About the Author 197

Introduction

In 1986, I opened my own private counselling practice. Today I am a counsellor, consultant, and facilitator, and I love what I do. I have a much better perspective on life and a greater understanding of people in general than I once did.

When I was 5 years old, my 14-year-old brother, Don, was killed by a hit-and-run drunk driver. My parents—my mom in particular—never recovered. My life changed that day. The loss of my brother was devastating, and because the family dynamics changed so dramatically, I felt like I had to grow up really quickly. That started me on a quest to understand people and discover why we do the things we do.

Most people have a tendency to interpret other people's behaviour based on how they do things themselves. For example, let's say you see two people from across a room, and one is speaking loudly to the other. If you speak loudly when you're angry, you may assume the person speaking loudly is angry. However, this may not be true at all. It could be that the person is speaking loudly because he or she is passionate about the topic of conversation. In general, people assume that others think, feel, or behave in the same way they do. But other people may simply process differently, and assuming otherwise can lead to misunderstandings and conflicts.

We all undergo uncomfortable communications or conflicts with others. For example, let's say Sue has been waiting for Larry to get home, and as soon as Larry walks through the door after work, Sue starts asking him questions about his day. Larry gets defensive, raises his voice, and asks, "Can't you give me a little space? Why are you giving me the third degree?"

Sue is hurt. Larry, who has what I will identify as cognitive in his communication zone, needs a transition period from his compartment at work to his compartment at home. Sue, who has kinesthetic in her communication zone, doesn't need this and is looking to connect with her partner because she hasn't seen him all day. With a little understanding of their processing styles, both of them could have their needs met.

We also all have times when we meet someone and it feels like we've known that person for a long time. Why is this so with some and not with others? The difference between uncomfortable communication and communication that flows smoothly and effortlessly could just be a difference in processing styles. Learning how to bridge these differences could be the answer you're looking for.

The PEP Personality Process is an excellent tool for gaining insight into the personality types of all the key people in your life: your spouse, children, bosses, co-workers, students, friends, and clients or customers. With it, you can discover what others expect from you in terms of communication and behaviour—and what you are expecting of them.

As you learn to adapt your communication and behaviour towards other people, even if they know nothing about processing styles, you'll make it easier for them to hear and understand you. Just imagine the relief of preventing misunderstanding and creating clarity!

Understanding the PEP Personality Process can help us in a variety of vital ways. The process:

- shows us how we learn and the best way for us to learn
- opens our eyes to our natural talents, abilities, and challenges
- helps us regain peace and move back into balance when we get stressed
- shows us how we interface with different environments and how they can affect us
- helps us understand our insecurities and what we can do about them

In short, it empowers us, helping us to make sense of our world and those in it.

Since the dawn of humankind, people have been seeking to know themselves and to understand each other better. Recognizing significant differences and particular patterns in human behaviour is nothing new. Five thousand years ago, the Egyptian and Mesopotamian civilizations used the elements of fire, water, earth, and air to determine personality traits. In the Bible, the prophet Ezekiel refers to the four faces of mankind.

More recently, the Myers-Briggs assessment, DiSC personality types, and Keirsey Temperament Theory have been used in business. I mention these because, in my journey to understand human nature, I've realized how important they have been not just to me but also to humanity. However, although I found them interesting and educational, I also found them lacking the completeness I was looking for. They did not answer all of my questions.

People are rich and layered, and they fascinate me. From a very early age, I wanted to know what made people tick. I was always asking questions and observing other people's behaviours. Exploring people's differences and similarities led me into my own spiritual, personal, and professional journey. In studying and learning NLP (neurolinguistic programming) and human psychology in conjunction with my spiritual explorations and personal experiences, I began to see patterns. Insights would come to me, and suddenly pieces would click into place. I would then test this inner knowledge with real people in my life. The more I worked with friends, students, groups, and clients, the more patterns emerged and pieces fit into place as a viable and useful way of profiling personality and behaviour. It has been a rewarding journey, and I look forward to sharing the PEP Personality Process with you.

This book is about taking responsibility for ourselves and how we interact with our world and the people in it. It's about valuing our differences as well as our similarities and building relationships with flexible, open, honest, and respectful communication. It offers a way to increase personal growth and assists us in living in a more balanced and effective way.

Part One
An Overview of the PEP Personality Process

Chapter 1
The PEP Personality Process

We are each born with a processing style. It doesn't come from our parents or our heritage. The way we process may be similar or totally different from our family members, which can explain so many dynamics within the family unit.

Our processing style involves four components and four zones. All of us have the same four components, with influence in each of the four zones. How we work through each of the components in the four zones determines many of our behaviours and actions, including

- how we filter information coming to us
- how we communicate with others
- how we handle stress
- what we do when we feel insecure
- how we understand or learn

All are affected by the four components and how they are arranged in the four zones—which, combined, make up your PEP Personality Process. I call it a *process* because we shift and change internally depending on what is happening at any given moment.

Understanding our PEP Personality Process gives us insights concerning our tendencies and those of others. It assists us in better knowing ourselves and understanding others, communicating more effectively, appreciating our differences, and better accepting each other. Before we get into how each component works in each zone, here is a brief explanation of the four zones as a foundational overview.

The Zones

Environmental
The environmental zone is where we first interact with our environment and where information first hits our senses before going inside our communication zone to be interpreted. How we first interact with the world often determines what we pay attention to in any given moment. Our senses can, at times, be overwhelmed by our environment.

Communication
The communication zone is all about how we communicate to ourselves and the world and how we receive communication from the world. It's about how we interpret the information coming to us and through us. It is the zone that determines how we make decisions. This zone is predominant and assists others in perceiving our personalities, since it is the face that we show most to the world. This is where our differences and similarities are often noticed first. It determines how we act and interact with people.

Challenge
The challenge zone works and blends closely with our communication zone. Often these two components and their characteristics and functioning blend, so that people might even think that the component in this zone is that of their communication zone. This blending adds richness and another dimension to our personalities. We use the component that is in the challenge zone as a secondary system, a backup check, or a final check for the decisions we are making.

It is called the challenge zone because when we have a physical or psychological stimulus that produces mental tension, or when we are stressed, this is the zone we shift into. When we are stressed, we tend to land hard internally in the out-of-balance qualities or challenges of the component in this zone. The component in this challenge zone and the out-of-balance qualities of that component are often magnified tenfold when we get stressed.

The component in our challenge zone is also where our personality will be most challenged by other people with this component in the communication zone—particularly when we are stressed or they are out of balance, because this reflects the personality traits that challenge us the most. It could be said that this zone and the component in it pose a major personal life challenge in the handling of this shadow side of our personality. It is probable that this is a part of our personality that we need to work on most to master in this lifetime.

Security

When we are not feeling confident or assured, or when we are fearful, we shift into our security zone. This is also the zone that we go into to create security in our lives. It's our safe place. It determines and influences how we react and respond when we are feeling insecure and go into the out-of-balance qualities of the component in this zone. When we are insecure, we often communicate and act from the out-of-balance tendencies of the component in this zone and the personality functions and characteristics of that component, both internally and externally. When we feel secure and are doing the things that create security for ourselves, the out-of-balance qualities are not present.

The Components

The four components are as follows:

1. Kinesthetic
2. Visual
3. Cognitive
4. Auditory

Each person has all four components, and how those four are situated in each zone determines how each component affects the personality. In the following chapters, we will explore the particulars of each component in each of the zones.

Going Out of Balance

When a person is out of balance, there are tendencies in each of the components that appear and come into operation. These tendencies can filter the information given and create specific types of behaviour, including problems, imbalances, and challenges. Some of us may think of these tendencies as our *shadow side* or *dark side*.

Our biggest shadow side may be in our challenge zone, but all of the components when they go out of balance, no matter what zone they are in, can cause us issues. When thinking about your out-of-balance state in each component and each zone, I encourage you to remember that for every problem or challenge, there is always a solution that can help you get back into balance. We can move back into balance with that component, in that zone, where we can then operate as our best self again.

Shifting Through the Zones

Each zone in our PEP Personality Process—communication, challenge, security, and environmental—is equally important as we shift from one zone to another throughout our day. For example, there may be times throughout our day when we are feeling stressed and shift into acting more from our challenge zone and the component that is there, or maybe we go into a situation that creates anxiety or a lack of confidence, and we shift into our security zone and start acting from the component that is there.

In each zone, the component and its personality function and characteristics have in-balance and out-of-balance tendencies. The way a person's needs, communication, talents, gifts, and challenges show up in the world is due to this shifting process, as are the characteristic tendencies revealed when a person is either in balance or out of balance in any of the components.

The process of shifting is determined by the communications coming at us and the communication we are sending, including all forms of communication both internal and external. It is also affected by our external or internal pressures or stresses, our internal state (i.e., feeling secure or not), and what is happening in our environment. This is why it is so important to know our own PEP Personality Processing style and that of others before jumping to conclusions. This understanding allows us to see what causes certain behaviours or tendencies and to act appropriately to create clear communication and ease of interaction when we encounter them.

The Diagram

The diagram that follows gives you a visual representation of the different zones and how we work through and with them. The outer zone represented by the house-shaped pentagon is the environmental zone. The circle is the communication zone. The square is the challenge zone, and the heart is the security zone.

Chapter 2
How to Assess Your Processing Style

If you're ready to experience more fulfilling relationships, increase your productivity, gain substantial self-knowledge, develop extraordinary people skills, and get the most out of this book and system, start with a self-evaluation, following the directions below.

I've found that the less you know ahead of time about the components and the zones that create the PEP Personality Process, the more accurate your answers to the questions will be. I have also found that the quicker and more intuitively you answer the questions, the better the results.

In answering the questions, remember that all of us have all four components, and you are to choose which is most like you most of the time, in most situations. That component would be a 4. Second most is a 3, third most is a 2, and least like you is a 1. There will always be exceptions, and it is important to look at it from this standpoint. Further, please realize that there are no right or wrong answers. Everything is based on your personal experience and what counts for you.

Knowing Me, Knowing You

PEP Personality Process—Self-Evaluation

Place a number next to each of the following statements. Each number can only be used *once* in each question. Use the following system to indicate your preferences:

> 4 = closest to describing me most of the time
> 3 = next-closest to describing me
> 2 = next like me
> 1 = least descriptive of me

Please answer all of the questions so each statement has a 4, 3, 2, and 1. Then, when you move to the scoring section of the evaluation, you will get accurate numbers.

1. **I communicate what is going on for me by**
   - __2__ using my words to give you the meaning of what I am saying.
   - __4__ emphasizing what I am telling you with the tone and volume of my voice.
   - __1__ sharing my feelings through my stories.
   - __3__ showing you my point of view.

2. **I naturally**
   - __4__ pick the most comfortable clothing or furniture.
   - __1__ gather information about things.
   - __3__ recognize voices I have heard before.
   - __2__ select colour combinations that look attractive together.

3. **I make important decisions based on:**
   - __3__ Does it look right?
   - __2__ Does it sound right?
   - __4__ Does it feel right?
   - __1__ Does it make sense?

4. **I tend to easily**
   - __4__ be sensitive and pick up on other people's feelings.
   - __2__ analyse situations and create logical solutions.
   - __1__ organize, plan ahead, and make lists.
   - __3__ work and talk at the same time.

5. I am influenced most in a debate or argument by
   __1__ the other person's reasoning.
   __2__ the other person's enthusiasm.
   __4__ the other person's intensity.
   __3__ the other person's perspective.

6. People respect me during a communication when they
   __4__ care about my feelings too.
   __2__ look me in the eye.
   __1__ listen to me without interrupting.
   __3__ are interested in my thoughts and reasoning.

7. On a project, I am more likely to first
   __1__ want to hear just the facts.
   __3__ want to see the overview.
   __2__ want to know what it is all about.
   __4__ want to have a solid grasp of why we are doing it.

8. To me, something is believable
   __2__ when I can see it clearly.
   __1__ when what I am hearing clicks.
   __4__ when I feel it in my gut.
   __3__ when I know it makes sense.

9. When I am challenged by a person, I find it most difficult
   __2__ to trust the person or situation.
   __1__ to be diplomatic and not get frustrated.
   __4__ to separate my feelings from what the other person is feeling.
   __3__ to be flexible and change my timing.

10. Describing myself, I'd say
    __1__ I am a logical person.
    __2__ I am a practical person.
    __4__ I am a people person.
    __3__ I am a punctual person.

Knowing Me, Knowing You

Scoring the Evaluation

Step One

Copy your answers from the self-evaluation questions to the lines below:

1. _2_ C   2. _4_ K   3. _3_ V   4. _4_ K   5. _1_ C
     _4_ A   _1_ C   _2_ A   _2_ C   _2_ K
     _1_ K   _3_ A   _4_ K   _1_ V   _4_ A
     _3_ V   _2_ V   _1_ C   _3_ A   _3_ V

6. _4_ K   7. _1_ A   8. _2_ V   9. _2_ C   10. _1_ C
     _2_ V   _3_ V   _1_ A   _1_ A   _2_ A
     _1_ A   _2_ C   _4_ K   _4_ K   _4_ K
     _3_ C   _4_ K   _3_ C   _3_ V   _3_ V

Step Two

Take the letters from step one and place the associated numbers in the proper column for each question. Then add the numbers in each column associated with each letter. There will be ten entries for each letter.

	V	K	A	C
1.	3	1	4	2
2.	2	4	3	1
3.	3	4	2	1
4.	1	4	3	2
5.	3	2	4	1
6.	2	4	1	3
7.	3	4	1	2
8.	2	4	1	3
9.	3	4	1	2
10.	3	4	2	1
Totals	25	35	22	18
	V	K	A	C

To check scores, add up V + K + A + C. They should equal 100.

Step Three

Transfer the totals for each letter into the "Your PEP Personality Process" graphic. The letter with the highest number goes in the communication zone. Next highest goes in the challenge zone. Next goes in the security zone, and the lowest-numbered letter goes in the environmental zone. The result will illustrate your PEP Personality Process.

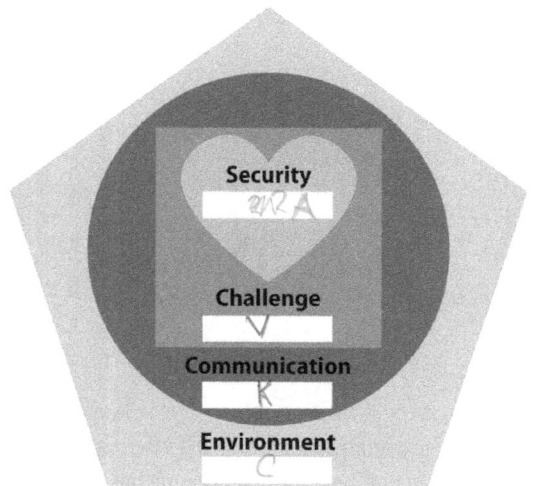

Your PEP Personality Process

The Components and a Tie Situation

If you have a tie, add only the first five numbers in your tied categories and place whichever is ahead before the other. For example:

V=24   K=25   A=25   C=26

For K and A only, add up the first five questions and place whichever is ahead before the other. So, if K is 12 and A is 9 by question five, then K goes before A in the PEP Personality Process self-evaluation.

In this example, the PEP Personality Process, from highest score to lowest, is C, K, A, V. In other words, the C component is in the communication zone, the K component is in the challenge zone, the A component is in the security zone, and the V component is in the environmental zone.

If you still have a tie after adding up the first five questions, look up each of the tied components in the appropriate sections of this book to determine which one is most like you in most situations. This is a little more challenging because of our own personal blind spots, so it may take some time to get it right. Sometimes it is easier for someone who knows you well to read over the descriptions and give you an opinion. After you have decided, continue to observe yourself or the person who had the tie until you are sure you are correct.

Many people ask me what it means if they fill out the self-evaluation again later and get a different result. Does that mean their processing style has changed? No. I have found that the first time you fill out the PEP Personality Process self-evaluation is the most accurate. If you fill it out again, quite often the results will be the same.

Chapter 3
How to Use This Book

One of the wonderful things about the PEP Personality Process is that it does not discriminate by culture, religion, country, sexual orientation, education, financial situation, or even gender. The processing styles apply to the individual as a human being on this incredible planet. All of us have a need to be accepted for who we are, to be understood, to feel secure, and to make sense of the world around us. We all want to be connected, heard, and seen, and to know we are loved.

Whether we know it or not, everyone has a processing style, and that processing style influences how our environment affects us, how we make decisions, how we interpret things, and how we react to situations. PEP Personality Processing styles are like the hardware in a computer or like the foundation that we as individuals have layered all the other information around. On the following pages, you'll find descriptions of each zone and each component in each zone. You'll also find numerous tips and tools for applying what you're learning to improve your communication and relationships, both personally and professionally.

Remember: it is to your advantage to determine your own PEP Personality Process by doing the self-evaluation and/or having the person you want to understand better do his or her self-evaluation before you read the descriptions.

Effective Use of This Book Starts with Yourself

The self-evaluation gives you the order of your components and how they fit into each of the four zones. To begin, look up the component in your environmental zone, then the component in your communication zone, followed by the component in your challenge zone, and finally the component in your security zone.

Pay close attention to the two most important components, which are in the communication and challenge zones. The traits of these components are the predominant characteristics in your interactions with others—for the most part, they reveal the face that you show to the world. Remember, though, that all of the components, in all of the zones, count and determine your personality tendencies.

I suggest that you thoroughly research each of your own four zones and the components in them. Learn about yourself first, be willing to look at your challenges, and use the tips throughout the book to become a master of your own challenges.

Utilizing This with Others

Once you have an understanding of your own processing style, I then suggest that to become more proficient with this model, you must have a firm comprehension and understanding of all four components in the communication zone. You will then begin to recognize them in others and can practice bridging your communication styles. This zone is the most visible part of our personality and so a good place to get started.

Notice the pace at which a person talks, as this will give you a clue to that individual's component in the communication zone. Notice the wording. One fun way to get good at recognizing wording is to concentrate on the words and phrases of each component at a time.

For instance, after studying words and phrases relevant to the kinesthetic communication zone, pick one day and only focus on the kinesthetic words you hear. Whenever you hear one, write it down. Make a list and see how many you noticed. After you've gained this awareness, it becomes easier to pick those words out.

Next, move on and do the same thing for visual words and phrases, then cognitive words and phrases, and finally auditory words and phrases. When you focus on one at a time, you will build awareness in all of them and can pick them out easily.

As you become proficient in recognizing which component is in the communication zone, you can then begin to understand how the blending of the components in the communication and challenge zones affect the personality of the person and how the secondary system or component in the challenge zone creates differences in personality.

Once you have a firm grasp of the communication zone and the challenge zone combinations and blending, start to understand and notice how the component in the environmental zone affects a person and can influence behaviour and personality as well. Because the environmental zone is the one people interface with first in any given situation, this is the system that can send individuals into overwhelm or give them their first impressions of you or the situation.

Last but certainly not least is the component in the security zone. This is the most difficult to discern by observation alone. If a person is very self-confident and secure, this component will not be visible, and the out-of-balance characteristics will only be seen rarely. On the other hand, if a person lacks confidence, has many areas of insecurity, or is going through a rough patch affecting self-esteem, it may seem like that individual is acting and behaving from the out-of-balance characteristics of the component in this zone a lot.

I do want to remind you that we need to take the whole PEP Personality Process into consideration, because there are twenty-four combinations which make up each of the twenty-four processing styles, and each has a distinct flavour and flare all its own. In this system, all of the zones and all of the components are active and dynamic. It is a model that can assist you in knowing each other well or just well enough to do business together. It can give you tools and ways to build deep and lasting relationships or friendships, and it can also be used to get along with your co-workers. This is incredibly useful in building and enriching relationships in business and in life.

Know that it does take some time and practice to recognize and work with the concepts and the different processing styles as well as their subtle differences, so be patient with yourself as you go. Wherever possible, get the other important people in your life to fill out the ten-question evaluation to determine what their actual PEP Personality Process is. This gives you a foundation for getting to know them and how to work, communicate, and build a better relationship with them.

As with any model, this one gives you certain perspectives and understandings. Please use it with the intent that I had in mind when I wrote the book: to assist people in knowing themselves, in knowing that others are and can be different than them, and in accepting that different is okay. Our differences can be complementary, and our strengths can support each other's. Our sameness often reflects back to us what we like or dislike about ourselves.

When we have the know-how and apply the learning, our understanding of our similarities and differences makes it easier to hear what others have to say, see their perspective, and grasp where they're coming from. This creates an atmosphere where people can accept each other and know how to handle situations more effectively. Making sense of our differences and being able to see where we can positively bridge with others is the key to creating more fulfilling and successful relationships.

Remember, we all have something to contribute—our gifts and natural talents. We all have challenges to master and overcome. There is no perfect processing style, although we will always have a bias for our own. The more we can know ourselves and know others; the more we can come from that place of acceptance, compassion, and gratitude; the more we can work towards win-win situations. Success begins with successful relationships.

The Benefits of Understanding the PEP Personality Process

Personally	Professionally
- More fulfilling relationships - Increased productivity - Reduced stress (stress management) - Identification of strengths (and how to use them) - Identification of challenges (and knowledge of what to do about them) - Improved motivation - Substantial self-knowledge	- Successful collaborations - Expansion of extraordinary people skills - Unlocked leadership potential - Better team-building skills - Ability to create rapport with anyone - Enhanced management skills - Improved ability to motivate self and others - Increased understanding of others

Part Two
The Environmental Zone

Read the description of this zone and then turn directly to your component or the component of the person who you want to understand better.

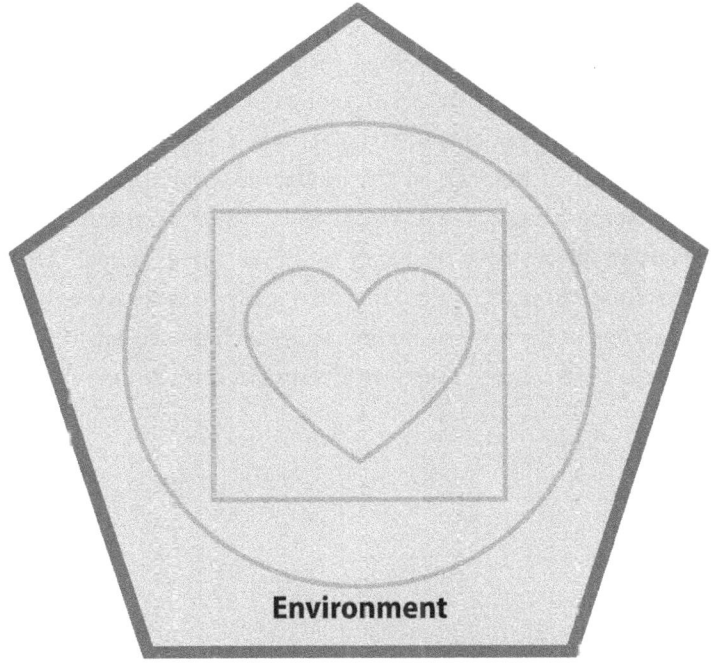

The environmental zone is all about how we interact with our environment. This is where we interface with the world and where information hits our senses. Our first experience in any environment will depend on which of the four components— kinesthetic, visual, cognitive, or auditory—predominates in this zone. Once our experience has been influenced by this component, it is then run through our communication zone to be interpreted.

Our style of interaction with the world often determines how we direct our attention in any given moment. Sometimes our senses can be overwhelmed by our environment, and sometimes, if we are focusing our attention elsewhere (such as internally), our environmental zone can be almost completely tuned out. Although this zone is important in gathering information, it is the least important system when it comes to making decisions. This is where we interface with our world, yet it is not as apparent in our personality as our other zones and the components in those zones.

The kinesthetic, visual, cognitive and auditory components can and do act differently in the environmental zone than in any of the other zones. We may be fooled into thinking that this is our communication zone, as it is the first responsive system.

Although it doesn't happen often, people can go out of balance in their environmental zone and display some of the out-of-balance qualities and functions of that component. Often, this is felt as a sense of overwhelm. Usually to go out of balance in the environmental zone, you would be triggered by something in the environment, or you would be in an out-of-balance state in all of the other zones first. Most people catch themselves and bring themselves back into balance in one of the other zones before they go out of balance in the environmental zone. If this does happen, the key is getting back in balance, and there are always effective strategies to assist us in doing that.

Chapter 4
The Environmental Zone: Kinesthetic

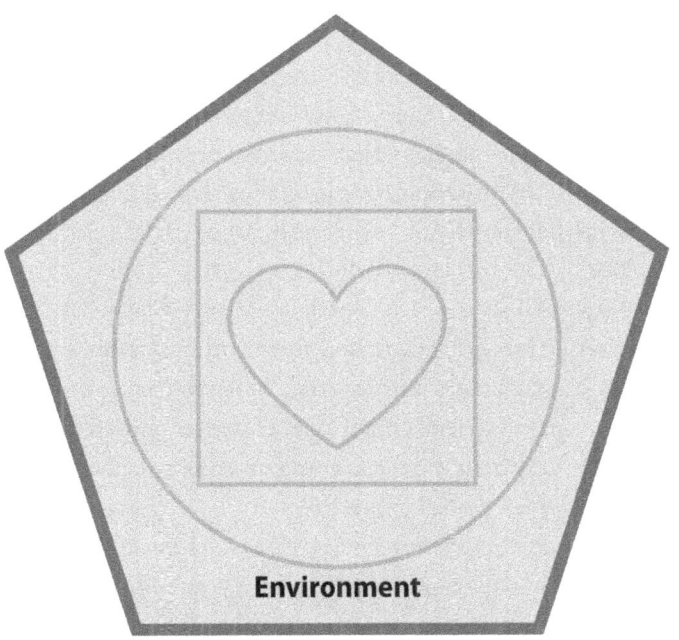

Kinesthetic is different in the environmental zone than in any other zone position because the interaction or interface with the world is through emotions, feelings, and touch. When we have this combination, the further away we are emotionally from another, the easier it is for us to pick up and interpret the person's feelings. The closer we feel emotionally with someone, the opposite is true. The feelings can often overwhelm us and send us into internal processing, which can make it appear that we are not being fully present in the moment with the person we care about.

In a primary relationship, people with kinesthetic in the environmental zone can often be overwhelmed by their partner's feelings. They tend to direct their attention internally, take things personally, and often totally miss what is going on for the other person at that time. Because they have been so internal and have viewed issues as being all about them, they can misinterpret what is happening.

This can lead other people to conclude that they are insensitive or selfish. But in actuality, they are overly sensitive and tend to take personally anything that is happening with those closest to them. A common complaint of someone close to a person with kinesthetic in the environmental zone would be, "Why can't you treat me as well as you did that other person, who you barely know?"

The reason they may appear to care more about mere acquaintances than their loved ones is that they do not perceive acquaintances as a threat to their emotional well-being, so they can interpret interactions clearly and act accordingly. With the people they love, they tend to go internal, interpret for self (look at what they think is the meaning of what is going on), and act from that place.

If they are feeling overwhelmed, they often want to close down communication or leave. Since this is the exact opposite of how a person with kinesthetic in their communication, challenge, or security zone would operate, it is confusing to those they love. However, with a little time away, these individuals may realize what is going on and come back and talk about it and work toward better understanding.

In NLP, we call this *sorting for self* or *sorting for other*. When you are sorting for self, your attention and focus is on yourself. You are inside your own head and paying attention to your thoughts, feelings, and ideas. When you are sorting for other, your attention and focus is out there on the other person—listening to that person's thoughts and picking up on their feelings and ideas.

Whereas people with kinesthetic in the communication zone, challenge zone, or security zone have a tendency to sort for other first and then sort for self, people with kinesthetic in the environmental zone have a tendency to sort for self first and then for other. People with kinesthetic in the environmental zone tend not to realize that they are doing this and are often confused when people think they're not sensitive. In fact, so much in their lives supports their belief that they are sensitive to others that this is difficult for them to believe.

At the same time, people with kinesthetic in the environmental zone do not take long to process emotional issues and are wary of decisions based in emotion, because emotions are not so much a part of their decision-making process. Most of the time, they enjoy physical touch from those they care about, although they can often forget to reciprocate. Many people with kinesthetic in the communication zone, challenge zone, or security zone prefer physical touch or contact, even during a disagreement. But a person with kinesthetic in the environmental zone could see physical touch during a time of disagreement as manipulative and may not want it for that reason.

To sum up, people with kinesthetic in the environmental zone tend not to handle emotionally intense communications well, particularly not with those who are closest to them. Often, they want to leave, emotionally or physically, or try to shut the other person down because they are going into overwhelm and cannot handle it.

Chapter 5
The Environmental Zone: Visual

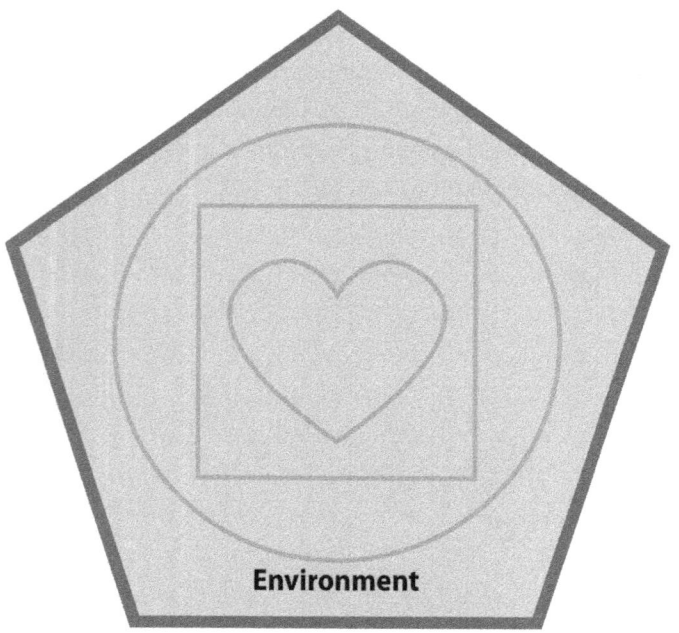

Visual is quite different in the environmental zone than in any other zone position because interaction or interface with the world is strongly influenced by the visual appearance of things and by the level of organization (or lack thereof) in our surroundings. With this combination, we can be overwhelmed by things being too disorganized in our environment or by having too many things on our to-do list. On the flip side, out of sight, out of mind—if we can't see it, we are largely unaffected.

People with visual in the environmental zone often have a critical eye and notice things in their environment. Many artists have visual in this zone. They can easily become overstimulated by visual things—movies, TV, computer, etc.—and need to be aware of this. When you are talking to them, if something is going on in the background visually, know that they may miss some of what you are saying because they are visually distracted.

People with visual in this zone, if the environment they are working or living in is very messy, may go into overwhelm and non-action. Or they will have to clean it up before anything else can get done.

Often people with visual in this zone will notice even small changes in facial expressions when people are talking to them, and this will be part of how they interpret the communication. Everything from their environment hits them in the visual sense first, so they see more than others do. Presenting things visually to this person will be useful. Because the visual is so important, people with visual in this zone feel frustrated if they cannot see things or have a clear view of what they are looking at.

Generally, people with visual in this zone will care about their appearance—unless, of course, they cannot see themselves, in which case they might not notice. This type works well with deadlines because they need a certain amount of time pressure to move into action. No deadline, and it may never get done.

People with visual in this zone tend to be more flexible than people who have visual in their communication, challenge, or security zones because this is not where they make their decisions. They tend to be a little more patient with others than people with visual in other zones—unless they themselves are under time pressure.

Chapter 6
The Environmental Zone: Cognitive

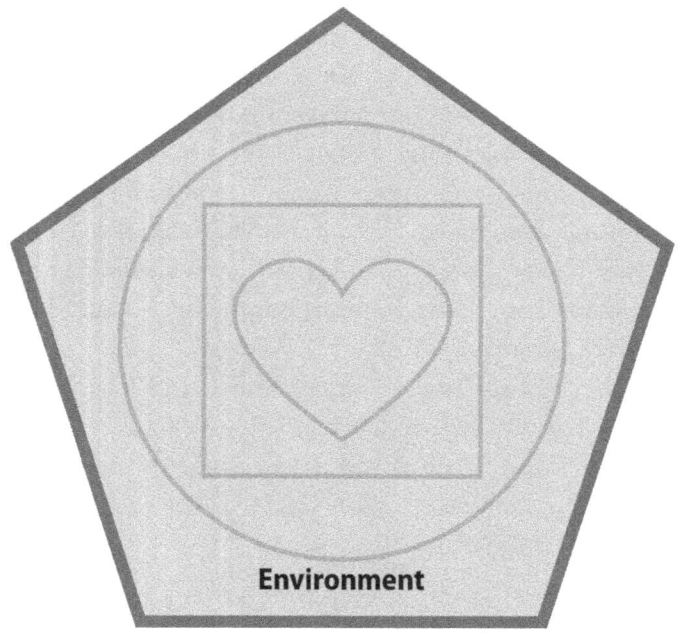

Cognitive is quite different in this zone than in any other zone position because the interaction or interface with the world is through words, sequence, logic, and inner knowing. With this combination, the way in which something is said to us is critically important because words and the sequence in which they are used will determine how we take in the information.

People with cognitive in the environmental zone have a tendency to hold on to the words others say and can get fixated on those words—sometimes giving them more importance than intended. To avoid confusion, the words coming at them verbally or in written form need to be sequential. For instance, if you are teaching these individuals something, saying "First you do ____, then next ____" will assist them in making sense out of what you are saying.

However, the way in which these individuals talk back to you may be a different story. They may not be sequential, logical, or take much care with their own words at all. So words coming at them hold a lot of importance to them, but their words in responding may not be well thought-out or given much importance.

The meaning you are giving things in your communication with these individuals or the meaning they are taking from what is going on in their environment affects them. Too many words coming at them at once or too much information at once can be confusing or overwhelming. Yet insufficient information could also be confusing. Words spoken or written that are out of logical sequence can also be confusing or overwhelming to them.

People with cognitive in the environmental zone will often pick up on things intuitively from their environment. They can pick up on things through their sense of inner knowing, and often they don't understand or realize how they have come to gain this knowledge about things going on around them. Strong smells can and will affect them; these can be stimulating or overwhelming. For example, wonderful food smells could be stimulating, but stinky garbage or dirty diapers could be overwhelming.

People with cognitive in this zone can take in information analytically, logically, and sequentially from their environment but do not necessarily express or communicate what they are thinking, feeling, or doing in that way.

Chapter 7
The Environmental Zone: Auditory

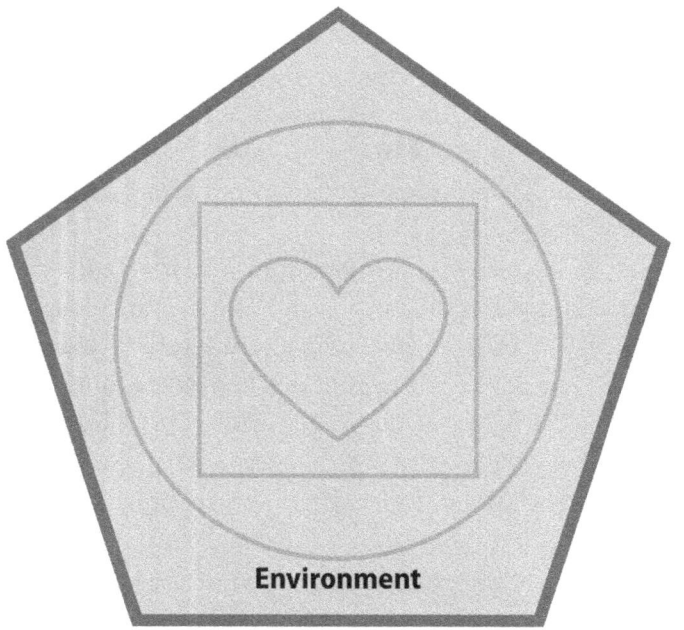

When auditory is in the environmental zone, our interaction or interface with the world is through sound. With this combination, we are acutely aware of the general quality of sound and changes in tone, inflection, or volume of voice.

People with auditory in the environmental zone usually want to listen to sounds or music of their own choosing and can get irritated by sounds in their environment that they have no control over. Poor quality of sound, such as a radio not quite tuned into the station, can really annoy or irritate them.

Music, talking, or sounds that are too loud or that have a volume above what is comfortable for them to listen to can overwhelm these individuals. They often like silence at least some of the time and prefer their work environment to be quiet or at least for the volume of sound to be at a low level.

People with auditory in the environmental zone are hypersensitive to being spoken to intensely and harshly or to being yelled at. Depending on the component in the communication zone, their reaction to this will differ. For example, a person with kinesthetic in the communication zone may shut down or get very emotional and even cry, while a person with cognitive in the communication zone may yell back or leave the situation. At a certain level of volume or loudness, this person may cease to hear the words and only hear them as noise or yelling.

Loud or sudden noises will have these individuals jumping out of their skin. They will jump more than another person, even if they know it is going to happen. For instance, even if they know someone is going to pop a bag, they will still jump anyway.

They can be over stimulated by sound and are more affected by the music in a movie, TV program, or drama than by what they are seeing. If they go into a bar or a situation where the music is way too loud for them, it can really affect them in a negative way. If they are prepared or the music is at a level they are okay with, they are fine.

People with auditory in the environmental zone prefer to hear information coming at them in a factual and direct way rather than beating around the bush. But paradoxically, often they do not communicate in that way themselves.

Part Three
The Communication Zone

Read the description of this zone and then turn directly to your component or the component of the person who you want to understand better.

The communication zone is about how we communicate with and interpret the world. It is also where we make our decisions. As such, it plays a major part in defining our personality.

In our professional and personal relationships, most of us experience personality conflicts from time to time. We may have difficulty creating rapport or feel personally offended by something another has done or said. On the other hand, most of us have enjoyed times when communication seems seamless, and we appear to be on the same wavelength without even trying. In both our working and personal lives, much rests on our ability to develop and maintain good positive relationships with others, even those we don't have that instant rapport with.

This section is designed to assist you in understanding and identifying differences in people's communication styles and personality traits influenced by the component in this zone. Remember that this is a major part of our personality, as it is through this component that we process and give meaning and understanding to the information coming to us. Through this component, we make our decisions and communicate to others. It is the face we show the world.

Through understanding human differences—including challenges, natural talents, and out-of-balance qualities—in the area of communication, we will be able to greatly improve our effectiveness in dealing successfully with others. Gaining an increased awareness of the four components in the communication zone will help you understand your boss, co-workers, family members, or partner. This awareness will help you discover what they expect from you as a person in terms of behaviour and communication—and vice versa. As you learn the skill of bending and bridging your communication style towards that of the person you wish to communicate with, you will find your relationships in the workplace and at home much easier.

Learning the four components in the communication zone and their characteristics—and how they affect a person's communication and behaviour—can improve how you communicate. Becoming self-aware of your communication style can assist you in bending and bridging so that the other person can understand you better. This knowledge could assist you in difficult situations that arise or help you avoid the difficult situation altogether.

Learning the skill of adapting yourself to these situations may take some effort on your part, but it is well worth it. For instance, even though I am not kinesthetic in my communication zone, I find that when I am speaking with a person who has kinesthetic in their communication zone, it serves me to talk in story form. This gives the person who has kinesthetic in their communication zone more of a feeling for what I am saying. If I was too direct or blunt, they might find it offensive, and the communication I was wanting to have would have gone sideways.

The chapters that follow give a detailed description of each of the four components and how they process and operate in the communication zone, as well as a description of the tendencies, behaviours, and qualities of each of the components. In summary, the communication zone is:

- how we communicate with, react to, and interpret our world
- where we make our decisions from
- the zone that influences how we learn best
- a major factor in how other people perceive our personality, since it presents the face and traits that we show the most
- where our differences and similarities are noticed first

Chapter 8
The Communication Zone: Kinesthetic

Unique Characteristics Overview

Because people with kinesthetic in the communication zone are emotionally based, emotionally sensitive, and tactile, they respond well to physical or emotional rewards, and they are dedicated and persevering when committed to what they are doing. People with kinesthetic in their communication zone are generally outgoing, friendly, conscientious, and good team players with huge empathy for others. They love having fun and being social—it makes life worthwhile.

People with kinesthetic in the communication zone naturally build relationships because they are nurturing, supportive, and loyal to those they care about. They can at times be very childlike and playful, for they maintain a sense of wonder, innocence, and sometimes naiveté no matter their age. They are generally optimistic and trusting and have a lot of patience, which assists them in always looking for the positive—the silver lining. However, these traits can cause them to stay longer than they should in situations that are not good for them. Since they tend to look for the good in everything and everyone, believing in the positive until proven otherwise, when things go wrong or don't turn out, they can feel betrayed.

If it feels right, people with kinesthetic in the communication zone can be flexible and spontaneous. When they get enthusiastic about something, they can be extremely animated and create enthusiasm in all around them. Because they are feeling their way through life, these individuals tend to grow up late—if they decide to grow up at all. They will often be later than others to find their niche in life, the right relationship, career, etc.

Those with kinesthetic in the communication zone often resist new things. Even if they do decide they want to do something new, they may decide to go slow, because they don't have a feeling for it yet. They can have a tendency to dwell in the past and relive past experiences, both positive and negative.

These individuals need to have fun; if it's not fun, they don't want to do it. They tend to laugh a lot and are full of love. They want to gain approval from those they care about, though they often create drama for attention.

People with kinesthetic in the communication zone prefer the tried-and-true methods of doing things. They like to have a blueprint for how things are done. This gives them a sense of solidity and confidence in whatever it is they are doing. At the same time, everything that happens to them—in their environments, with people, in learning—is evaluated based on how it *feels* to them. Comfort is their top value and a huge need; comfort in their clothing, environment, relationships, and all situations is extremely important. In any area of their lives, if those with kinesthetic in their communication zone are not comfortable, they can get irritable and moody.

Feeling is most important with these people, both emotionally and physically. They respond according to how it feels and whether it feels right or not. For other processing styles—which rely more on making sense and logic, how it sounds, and facts, plans, and pictures—acting just because "it feels right" is often a foreign concept.

Communication

People with kinesthetic in the communication zone process externally, which means they like to talk everything through, out loud, giving details and telling stories—the purpose of which is to give the listener a feeling for what they are saying. When telling a story, it is important to them that they finish, because they are processing as they talk. Other types may get frustrated with all the details and just want them to get to the point.

People with kinesthetic in the communication zone generally move and talk more slowly than others, often pausing to go inside during conversation. They are soft-spoken—unless upset. They often talk more slowly, and their speech sometimes sounds breathy. They pause as they speak because they are going inside to find words that match their feelings. Bouncing their feelings off the person they are talking to helps them understand what it is they are truly feeling.

When listening to someone else, they ask many questions because they need more detail to get a feeling for the topic. Some of their questions may seem redundant or obvious to other personality types, but those with kinesthetic in the communication zone may just need to hear it said in a different or more detailed way. When they ask questions, even if the questions seem trivial, they do need an answer—it helps them get a feeling for things. Often, just expressing their feelings out loud in words will help them arrive at a resolution, and they will have no need to discuss it further.

At times, those with kinesthetic in the communication zone cannot find the right words or will find it difficult to put their feelings into words. At these times, they may not be willing to talk—or if they do talk, they may just throw out words until they can find the ones that fit. This can be confusing to people they are communicating with and may create misunderstandings. When they feel strongly about something or are upset, expressing emotion and emoting while communicating is a given for the person with kinesthetic in the communication zone. They readily share their kindness and affection and will frequently choose to stand close to others when talking to them, often touching them to emphasize a point or to feel connected while communicating.

They like to express their sentiments but will go out of their way to avoid hurting someone else's feelings—often at the expense of their own. They readily engage in physical affection and embracing, and they do it simply because they like to express their genuine feelings of tenderness and caring. If others use loud, sarcastic, or harsh tones of voice, it will cause a strong emotional response and what has been said may not be heard or may be misinterpreted.

Words often used to describe the person with kinesthetic in the communication zone include:

- compassionate
- demonstrative
- emotional
- emotive
- generous
- humble
- joyful
- optimistic
- patient
- playful
- popular
- sensitive
- sociable
- soft-hearted
- spontaneous
- supportive
- talker
- trusting
- warm

Language

Each component in the communication zone has its own language. Those with kinesthetic in the communication zone will use more of the kinesthetic language than those who have a different component in that zone.

Speech Patterns

Often the person with kinesthetic in the communication zone will use long, complicated sentences and tell stories with extensive detail. Why? You guessed it—they want to give you a *feeling* for what they're talking about. All action, emotional, and tactile words or phrases are kinesthetic language. These words will frequently show up when these individuals are talking. When you use the same words, it will help them in understanding you better. Typical words and phrases include the following:

Emotions
- afraid
- aggravated
- agitated
- angry
- annoyed

- anxious
  - bashful
  - bored
  - calm
  - cherish
  - depressed
  - distressed
  - enthusiastic
  - envy
  - excited
  - fear
  - frustrated
  - glad
  - gloomy
  - guilt
  - happy
  - hateful
  - heartfelt
  - hope
  - hurt
  - joy
  - love
  - passionate
  - sad
  - shame
  - sympathetic
  - upset

Tactile
- alert
- alive
- balance
- blow
- breathless
- bumpy
- catch
- close
- cold
- comfortable
- concrete
- connect
- contact
- deep
- distance
- endurance
- energy
- faint
- feel
- firm
- fit
- full
- grasp
- handle
- hard
- heavy
- hungry
- light
- numb
- over
- press
- pulsing
- quick
- quiver
- rough
- rub
- scrape
- sensory
- shallow
- sharp
- slow
- smooth
- soft
- solid
- stand
- stir
- strike
- strong
- support
- throb
- tingle
- touch
- tremble
- under
- unmoving
- warm
- weak
- anything to do with tactile or the physicality of something or someone

Action
- absorbing
- acting
- affection
- busy
- caring
- comforting
- courageous
- daring
- eagerness
- emotional
- encouraged
- entertaining
- exercise
- flowing
- fun
- impression
- jump

- kind
- leap
- lively
- manipulative
- movement
- panting
- playful
- playing
- pleasure
- practice
- readiness
- running
- sensitivity
- spread
- suffer
- sulky
- surprised
- swimming
- tenderness
- tense
- thankful
- thrill
- underhanded
- unfeeling
- walking
- zeal
- all actions and action words

Phrases
- all washed up
- bite off more than you can chew
- blow off steam
- boils down to
- catch on
- chip off the old block
- come to grips with
- connect with
- control yourself
- cool, calm, and collected
- don't spread yourself too thin
- finger on the pulse
- fire it up
- firm foundation
- get a handle on
- get a hold of
- get a load of this
- get the drift of
- go-getter
- hand in hand
- hang in there
- hold it
- hold on

- keep your shirt on
- know the ropes
- lay the cards on the table
- moment of panic
- moved by
- on one's toes
- on the go
- on the rocks
- pain-in-the-neck
- pass over
- pitch in
- pull some strings
- put your best foot forward
- rubs me the wrong way
- sharp as a tack
- slip through
- smooth operator
- start from scratch
- stiff upper lip
- tap into
- topsy-turvy
- touch base
- touch upon
- turn around
- walk through

In Business

When you want to present your product, proposal, or point of view to the person with kinesthetic in the communication zone, for optimum understanding and consideration, take a slower, considerate tone—and show some enthusiasm. Also, using their kind of language assists them in understanding what you are saying. When you use their language, it fits for them and is more comfortable. If you can give them a hands-on demonstration, it's even better.

Metaphors or stories assist these individuals in getting a feeling for what you are discussing. So telling a story about the product or people using the program will assist them in understanding. Providing examples of others who were satisfied with the proposal or who are recommending your program, proposal, or product also assists them in creating a feeling for what you are talking about. This helps them in making a decision about it. For example, you might say: "If I could *walk* you through it, you could get a better *feeling* for it, couldn't you?" or "If this *feels* right to you, I will go ahead and handle the paperwork. So then you too can be *satisfied* and *happy* like Mrs Robertson."

Personal Interactions

In personal interactions with people with kinesthetic in the communication zone, it's helpful to reflect back to them the feeling you are getting from what they are saying. For example: "It sounds like you had a really enjoyable time visiting your friend in Calgary. You did lots of fun things!" or "It sounds like that really upset you, and you feel like you need to do something about it." It's important to listen to their stories and show interest.

Important Question

Why? is the most important question for people with kinesthetic in the communication zone. Understanding why they are doing something gives them the feeling and direction they need and the motivation to do it. But they also need to be careful with how they use *why* questions, as such inquiries can lead to a serious emotional wallow.

For example, asking "Why am I feeling this way?" can assist the person with kinesthetic in the communication zone in discovering valid information. But questions like "Why does this always happen to me?" or "Why can't I do it?" often create a situation where the unconscious mind is giving them answers to questions based on their past experience, which takes them into the mire of their negative thoughts and puts them in danger of getting lost in a wallow.

Learning

Those with kinesthetic in the communication zone are action-oriented, tactile, enthusiastic team players who learn best with hands-on training. They learn by methodically doing or walking through something, usually several times, which gives them a feeling and understanding for it and assists them in remembering the steps. Making things fun creates a good learning environment for them.

Getting a feeling for what they are learning takes up more neurology; therefore, it takes more time in the beginning for the person with kinesthetic in the communication zone to "get it". However, once they have done so, they really do have it. Being action-oriented, they would rather just jump in and start doing things and skip the instructions, lecture, demonstration, or (in their mind) laborious planning or researching process.

Telling them stories which engage their feelings also assists them in learning. They love detailed information because it gives them a feeling for what it is you are teaching them. Once they've walked through something a few times and have learned it experientially, they can do it again and again.

The person with kinesthetic in the communication zone needs to take the time to feel things through—to process. Because of this, school systems have at times mislabelled them as slow learners. This is totally inaccurate. The speed of processing and the need for experiential learning has nothing to do with intelligence. The person with kinesthetic in the communication zone is just as intelligent as anyone else.

It is important to give the person with kinesthetic in the communication zone time to respond and get a feeling for learning. These individuals memorize by doing or walking through something. In a classroom setting, students with kinesthetic in the communication zone may stick out because of their constant need to move. Their high levels of energy may cause them to be agitated, restless, and/or impatient. For the person with kinesthetic in the communication zone, memory and learning are strengthened by the use of their own body's movements. They will be interested in what "feels right" or gives them a "gut feeling".

People with kinesthetic in the communication zone are rarely still, because the movement or fiddling helps them to process. This is the second reason why they tend to move a lot; the action helps them learn. This is important for parents, teachers, and facilitators to understand.

It is especially important for these individuals to feel comfortable and have a certain amount of social interaction. Personal relationships are extremely important to people with kinesthetic in the communication zone, and they need to feel connected to the group. They take the time they need to settle into their environment and are often *nesters*—people who make sure they have all their creature comforts around them and make themselves as comfortable as possible.

Major Personality Challenges

The major personality challenge for people with kinesthetic in the communication zone is having boundaries and setting boundaries. They are profoundly emotional, tend to take everything personally, and are easily hurt. They are extremely sensitive and often pick up on other people's feelings and moods, even when these are not obvious. Because they are so sensitive to others, setting boundaries is a major challenge. They fear that saying no or being really direct may hurt another's feelings, and they try to avoid that. Sometimes it is challenging for these individuals to discern where they begin and end, what their boundaries are, and even whose feelings they're feeling. This can affect their decision-making.

Career/Organizations

Generally, those with kinesthetic in the communication zone do their best as team players. If they are leaders or managers, they like to manage by consensus. They usually don't want the full responsibility, are overly concerned by what others may feel, and don't like to give orders that others may not appreciate. They can be excellent leaders in positions that are more about group consensus and where they are still considered part of the team.

These individuals are loyal, dedicated, and persevering in whatever causes they are involved in. They are action-oriented. They are good workers who have the ability to act and get things done. Provided they have enough socializing and fun on the job, they will be positively motivated, hard workers. They are excellent at following instructions once they have a feeling for the project and are absolutely conscientious about their work.

They are skilled but sometimes may feel challenged in organizing details, depending on whether they are in or out of balance. The person with kinesthetic in the communication zone generally responds better to physical and emotional rewards and praise because it feels good to get rewarded and singled out for a job well done. With harsh criticism or threats, they will often make more mistakes or have more sick days because they take everything personally and it is too uncomfortable.

Excessive conflict will cause these individuals to quit a job or leave a situation. When people with kinesthetic in the communication zone are happy on the job, they are willing and easy to work with and exceptionally helpful, for they are people-people. They have a natural affinity and caring for others.

Amusement and Humour

People with kinesthetic in the communication zone usually like life-related humour (funny things that people do) and slapstick humour. They can feel very hurt if they are the butt of a joke, which sometimes happens because of their trusting and naïve nature. Compared with the other communication styles, it can take longer for people with kinesthetic in the communication zone to really get a joke. They may laugh at the time, enjoying other people's enjoyment, or it may seem as if the joke has slipped by them. They may ask a question to get more of a feeling for the joke, which can cause others to laugh and hurt their feelings. Often later, after having felt the joke through, they will have a laugh to themselves. So sometimes they get two laughs from one joke—one at the time of telling and one later when they really understand it.

Decisions

It's important for people with kinesthetic in the communication zone to take the time they need to make a decision and get the right kind of feeling about the decision they are making. They make their best decisions from their gut feelings about things. They have an incredible ability to feel a situation and to become a part of it. This can be a major advantage in understanding the situation, but it can at times lead them to be swayed by other people's feelings, opinions, and actions.

Too often, because they are sensitive to what other people want and feel, if you put them on the spot to make a decision, people with kinesthetic in the communication zone will end up giving the answer that the other person wants to hear. Then, after feeling the decision through, they find it is not an answer they are comfortable with or the decision they wanted. At this point, they either have to go back and change their decision—which looks like they are changing their minds—or do the thing they don't want to do and probably resent doing it. Or they may cope by not getting around to doing it, or by avoiding it altogether.

Therefore, it is really important for those with kinesthetic in the communication zone to give themselves time to make the right decision. One way of delaying their response is to say something like, "I'll get back to you tomorrow morning" or "I'll let you know by the end of this hour." Such phrases help them get some time away from the person who is asking them to make the decision, so they can feel it through for themselves. This ensures that they are happy and comfortable with the decision they make.

It may happen that the person with kinesthetic in the communication zone becomes overwhelmed by too many choices and has too much to feel through. If these individuals receive too much information, they may seek solitude to process. This is particularly true if a conflict comes up. It is as if they get full with feelings and information. They can't take in any more until they work through what they have already been exposed to. Trying to make them listen to you after this has happened is like trying to put more water in an already overflowing jug.

Physical Space

In their physical environment, people with kinesthetic in the communication zone are settlers or nesters and have a tendency to have piles: piles of paper, piles of clothes, etc. These may be neat piles or not-neat piles, but there will be piles. They also usually have more memorabilia or knick-knacks than others. Sentimental or cute objects get more attention.

With furniture, comfort is usually more important than looks—or an item can look good as long as it feels really comfy. Remember, comfort is king when it comes to the person with kinesthetic in the communication zone.

Physiology

Breathing

Observing people with kinesthetic in the communication zone, you'll notice their breathing is full-bodied, causing the stomach to go in and out. They will typically be breathing from the bottom of the lungs, so breathing is deeper and slower.

Movement

In general, the movement of people with kinesthetic in the communication zone is slower unless they are excited. They generally move and talk more slowly than others and often pause as they speak. Usually if they are telling a story or expressing strong feelings, they are quite expressive physically and get right into the feeling of whatever topic they are speaking on, which can give them more colour in their skin tone.

They are often physically responsive when they are talking; they may reach out and touch your arm or give you a hug. When shopping or looking at things, they will often reach out and touch or feel the item. They are noticeably tactile in their approach.

Most of the time, they do not like to sit still, particularly for longer periods. They need movement to assimilate information, so as a rule they move around, fidget, and touch things more than other communication styles.

Gestures

People with kinesthetic in the communication zone can re-enact a story as they tell it to you, engaging all of their feelings, actions, and behaviours as if they were literally reliving it. It is as if their whole body is engaged in recreating the story. When they are not telling a story, their gestures during speech are generally below the waist.

Physicality

Kinesthetic communicators are more aware of their physical bodies and tend to feel physical discomfort and pain more keenly than other personality styles. They are generally physically agile, with good balance and good mind-body coordination. They usually have good manual dexterity and enjoy working with their hands. However, they can manifest their stresses and emotions in a physical way by becoming ill or getting a headache or stomach ache.

They respond to physical and emotional rewards and touching, and as noted earlier, they stand closer to people than other personality styles. They are the ones in the supermarket who you see squeezing the tomatoes or in a clothing store touching the fabric to have that physical experience.

Out-of-Balance Tendencies

When people with kinesthetic in the communication zone go out of balance, they begin to take everything personally. What is said, other people's reactions to things, other people's behaviours—they may feel that literally anything that is happening around them is about them or directed at them. They can become dramatic, defensive, or clingy. They require constant reassurance, and if they don't get it, they become discouraged. They don't accept responsibility for themselves and can act helpless and uninformed in order to gain sympathy. They can also go into an emotional wallow or pity pot—as the line from the children's songs goes: "Nobody likes me, everybody hates me, I think I'll go eat worms."

These individuals are acutely sensitive, and when they express that outwardly, it can look to other people as if they are feeling sorry for themselves, complaining, whining, or wimping out. But usually what is happening is that they are working through or trying to get a handle on what they are feeling and why. They need to talk it out because they process externally. This kind of processing can start out sounding negative.

If they have the opportunity to become emotional and talk their issues out loud to someone who gives them an empathetic ear, they can work through their emotions and get out of the wallow or negative feelings. They do not necessarily have to understand what it is about. Sometimes just expressing the emotion is enough to process it.

When people with kinesthetic in the communication zone feel bad, they want everyone around them to feel bad. Therefore, they can be quite manipulative or at times overly dramatic. This is where the saying "misery loves company" comes from.

Because these individuals are more in their physical body than others, they can create physical symptoms or even dis-eases more readily than others. These may include stomach aches, pains, or even physical injuries.

Often when people with kinesthetic in the communication zone are out of balance, they become childish. If they are hurting—for real or imagined reasons—they will strike out verbally or physically to hurt another without any thought as to the consequences. Most of the time, what is said or done is later regretted.

More than one person with kinesthetic in the communication zone has been described by others as having a tantrum. Sometimes when they are out of balance, these individuals will deliberately create chaos in order to bring attention to themselves. Usually, their purpose in dumping their emotional stuff is to create an opportunity to process. They want reassurance, to connect, and to have physical closeness or affection. They want the discomfort to stop at almost any cost.

They also have a tendency to stay in their suffering until *they* are ready to come out of it—so attempts to make them feel better before they are ready to feel better often fail. It is important to recognize that these people need time to feel things through. Giving them the space and time to do so is respectful, because it actually does take them longer. Their processing involves more neurology than with other personality styles.

Another way to assist people with kinesthetic in the communication zone in coming back into balance is to quit talking. Excess words only add to the pile of things they have to feel through. When they are full of emotion and information, they can't take any more in. They will only want to get away from the situation.

When people with kinesthetic in the communication zone are out of balance, they tend to be non-active. They begin to come back into balance when they start to take action again. Also, they respond well to simple physical affection without complicated words; this will speak louder to them. Reconnecting with those they care about and also having fun are good ways for them to get back into balance. Remember that comfort, fun, and action are key for the person with kinesthetic in the communication zone.

Review of Kinesthetic in the Communication Zone

Highest Values

- comfort
- fun

Needs

- harmony in relationships
- time to process
- to be social; to be around and with people
- to be taking action in their lives to stay in balance
- fun, fun, and more fun
- comfort in all things
- to move physically
- to express emotionally
- to talk things through

Challenges

- being overly emotional
- discernment:
  - Where do I begin and end?
  - Are those my feelings or someone else's?
- boundaries—knowing where they are and setting them as needed
- saying *no*

How Others Describe Them

- caring
- charming
- childish
- demonstrative
- drama queen
- emotional
- friendly
- fun-loving
- giver
- manipulative
- nurturer
- overly emotional
- people-person
- playful
- popular
- promoter
- social
- spontaneous
- talker
- theatrical
- touchy-feely
- way too sensitive

Out-of-Balance Behaviours

- taking everything personally
- being overly emotional
- getting defensive and clingy and requiring constant reassurance
- failing to take responsibility
- dwelling upon a negative feeling (the "wallow")
- feeling sorry for self (the "pity pot")
- complaining, whining, or wimping out
- being manipulative or at times overly dramatic
- creating physical symptoms or even dis-eases
- acting childish/dramatic
- disorganizing situations to create attention
- staying in their suffering until they are ready to come out
- wanting to leave when they are full of emotion and can't take in any more
- procrastinating and not taking action

Solutions to Create Balance

- talking it out
- action, action, action
- fun, fun, fun
- time alone to feel things through
- reconnecting with those they care about
- physical affection without confusing words

Chapter 9
The Communication Zone: Visual

Unique Characteristics Overview

People with visual in the communication zone have an innate sense of balance and symmetry. They are often intellectual and artistic, and they appreciate beauty, nature, and making things look good. They have a natural ability to see what it is like to walk in another person's shoes and so realize the importance of not imposing on others. This helps them establish rapport and good communication with others and assists them in being able to work with others easily.

People with visual in the communication zone are especially concerned with how things look: how they look themselves, how their environment looks, the look on the face of the person who is talking to them, and the appearance of their family or spouse and how that reflects on them. This is how they interpret the world. Understanding is based on seeing a clear picture of the subject. They also believe that others will value them based on visual criteria. With friends, outward manifestations of affection that they can see are important (hugs, gifts, notes, dates set for get-togethers).

An amusing aspect is that people with visual in the communication zone quite often don't believe that they are visual. They seem to not be aware of their process of rapidly forming pictures or mental movies. Because it is so quick and easy for them, they often can't perceive that they actually do this.

People with visual in the communication zone, with their love of beauty and order, believe that everything has its right place and that it should be in that place. They need to be in environments that are aesthetically pleasing to them. If the environment is really out of harmony or disorganized, they can get irritated or even overwhelmed. They think in pictures, and so they will visualize everything you are saying. If you are talking about something that creates a picture they don't like or grosses them out, they may well ask you to stop.

Those with visual in the communication zone have a good critical eye, and everything comes under scrutiny to see if it fits with their picture of the world and how they think it should be. They are generally well coordinated in their choice of colour and style of clothing and accessories. Appearances are important to them, and so they are well-groomed, clean, and orderly. They tend to be self-conscious about the way they look and also about how others who are with them look.

In everything they do, people with visual in the communication zone demand the highest standards of excellence from themselves and others, and they can have difficulty accepting that others do not have the same standards—or have different ones. They process information very quickly and can easily see the big picture of how things will look. This sometimes makes them impatient with those who process more slowly.

They are highly intellectual and value this quality in others. They are usually academically oriented and high achievers in school. People with visual in the communication zone are particularly rule-governed. They play by the rules and expect that others will also. They have a strong sense of right and wrong, and their judgements can appear quite black-and-white at times, with little or no grey in between.

They are excellent at organizing and planning, with lists, lists, and more lists. The person with visual in the communication zone has lists for everything and doesn't merely *like* checking things off the list but *loves* it. These individuals have a natural ability for timelines, organization, and planning. Time and the timing of things are absolutely important to them. They like to know when something is happening so they can plan and look forward to it. Punctuality is noticeably important to them. They like things to begin and end on time, and if they are in charge, things certainly will.

Having events, goals, or plans to look forward to is critical to people with visual in the communication zone. If they don't have things to look forward to, they can get bored, depressed, or out-of-sorts. The anticipation and planning of something like a holiday, for example—getting the brochures, imagining the things they will do, researching the country, finding people and places to see—will be almost as pleasurable for them as the holiday itself.

When it's time for people with visual in the communication zone, it's really *time*. Time is a ruling force in their life. They are driven to move according to their own timing, which of course may be different from that of others. They may unknowingly put time pressure on those around them.

I once counselled a couple in which he was visual in the communication zone and she was kinesthetic in her communication zone and visual in her security zone. Both had the same starting time for work and were trying to commute together in order to avoid taking two cars. He liked to get to work an hour before he had to start so that he could have a coffee, get organized, and plan his day. She liked to get to work only ten minutes ahead of her start time; she felt both very pressured to go to work early and judged as being wrong for not wanting to do this.

Every morning he would ask her to hurry up because he was feeling stressed at not getting there as early as he wanted. She would get resentful and stressed because she had to speed up her own natural timing to accommodate him (or felt like she did). So both of them weren't getting their needs met.

In the end, they understood that the problem lay in their different outlooks, and they decided that it was okay to be different. They chose not to continue commuting together, which allowed them both to be more relaxed in their morning routines. This simple change—once they understood what was going on—saved their relationship from having this unnecessary stress.

As a general rule, people with visual in the communication zone are morning people. They like to be up early to get a good start on the day. They are often cheerful, happy, and wide awake in the morning and are not totally understanding of people who don't share this trait.

In order to really believe they are loved, people with visual in the communication zone need to be visibly shown love and affection. Gifts, notes, being seen together, doing things for them which are easily seen, physically hugging them, and giving special looks are some ways to make them feel loved.

As a general rule, these individuals are more traditional than those with other personality styles. If they haven't adopted family or cultural traditions, they will create their own. Or they will adopt others who fit with their picture and take pleasure in living by those.

Keeping a visual record of events is especially important to the visual communicator. The old saying "a picture is worth a thousand words" is so true for them—that image will pull up all the thoughts and feelings of that moment and take them right back to it. They like to have photo albums full of their good times, special people, vacations, and special events.

Patience is something that all the people with visual in the communication zone are working on or need to, because others often don't pick up on their pictures or plans as quickly as they do. Often, they get impatient because they don't realize that others are different and need more time, details, or facts. When other people are talking to them, they really want just the overview or the big picture. From their point of view, the details are only important if needed.

Communication

People with visual in the communication zone like to be seen and recognized—as long as it's in a positive light. They can at times be quite dramatic in their look or their presentation. They like to be the centre of attention, although it can be nerve-wracking for them. They don't like being put on the spot unprepared. They hate looking like a fool. Neither do they take criticism well; even constructive criticism is hard for them, as they are perfectionists.

Usually they make great facilitators or coaches because they have such a clear vision and can assist others in visualizing goals. Sometimes when communicating, they can see the picture so clearly themselves that they leave out important details, often assuming everyone has the same clear vision of it as they do. Then they can be quite disappointed later when they find out that they weren't understood or the picture they had in mind wasn't realized.

They can get frustrated when they communicate what they want or need and people don't get the picture right away. It is important when communicating or working with the person with visual in the communication zone to ask questions and backtrack as needed to clarify and pick up any missing pieces of the picture or plan that the individual may have unknowingly left out.

Often when people with visual in the communication zone are talking, they are focused on their own movie or picture. They may have no ears for what you are saying. If you want them to hear, make sure you have their attention and look them in the eye before speaking. Similarly, if you are talking to them and they have a fixed picture or have been triggered into their own movie, they may not hear you.

In school, children with visual in the communication zone are often the ones who are sent for hearing tests, as they can appear to be extremely selective in their listening, particularly if they are not being taught in a way that engages them (in which case, daydreaming can also often be an issue). However, their apparent inattention does not usually affect their grades, as they pick things up very quickly. This behaviour could just be a sign of boredom.

When someone is communicating a new way of doing something or a new idea to people with visual in the communication zone, they will usually at first say no. Other processing styles might take this at face value, but in actual fact, most first time *no* responses from people with visual in the communication zone are really their way of saying, "No, I can't visualize that" or "No, I have a different picture, and I haven't gotten enough information to form a new picture yet." This tendency can often get them labelled as stubborn, rigid, or inflexible.

So then when people with visual in the communication zone come back a while later and say "Yes, let's do that" or "I think that's a great idea," they are often met with disbelief, having already said no—and maybe even several times! But now that they have had time to mull it over and their picture has changed, they are ready and happy to do it the new way.

It's vital to understand that the person with visual in the communication zone needs time and information to change pictures, particularly if a fixed image about something has already been developed. The moment people with visual in the communication zone change the picture, their attitude and response change as well. It can be an almost instantaneous change. Other personalities are not like this and sometimes have a hard time believing that the person with visual in the communication zone—who was before so seemingly opposed to something—is now so completely okay with it. The shift can be viewed with distrust, disbelief, or just plain confusion.

If you want to change plans with a person with visual in the communication zone, tell them ahead of time so they can adjust their timing, picture, and plans. Last-minute changes are a real challenge for them.

Language

Speech Patterns

The speech of people with visual in the communication zone tends to be slightly fast and excited—and the more excited they are, the faster it gets. Often these individuals will use quickly assembled words with a minimum of detail and assume that you have grasped the same picture or movie that they have.

All descriptive words, colours, and visually sensed (external or internal) words or phrases are the language of the visual communicator. Typical words and phrases include the following:

About the eyes
- 3-D
- blind
- eyesight
- far-sighted
- nearsighted

- sight
- vision

Descriptive internal visual
- brilliance
- dawn

- envision
- flashy
- illuminate
- imagine
- insight
- reflect

- shining
- showy
- visualize

The act of sight
- appear
- focus
- gaze
- glance
- glimpse
- illustrate
- imagine
- look
- observe
- peep
- picture
- reveal
- scan
- see
- show
- squint
- stare
- survey
- view
- watch

Quality of the picture
- bright
- clear
- coloured
- colourful
- colourless
- contrast
- dark
- dim
- dull
- faded
- focused
- foggy
- framed
- gleam
- glisten
- glitter
- hazy
- hue
- iridescence
- light
- pale
- panoramic
- shade
- sparkling
- tint
- tunnel vision
- twinkle
- un-faded
- unframed
- vivid

Descriptive external visual
- beam
- display
- dreamer
- flash
- glow
- illustrate
- image
- mirage
- moonlight
- movie
- outlook
- reflection
- scene
- splendour
- sunlight
- viewpoint
- vista

All colours
- beige
- black
- blue
- bronze
- brown
- gold
- green
- grey
- orange
- pink
- purple
- red
- silver
- violet
- white
- yellow
- other shades of colour, such as light blue, dark blue, indigo, turquoise

Phrases
- a look-see
- a shade of
- all the colours of the rainbow
- an eyeful
- appears to me
- at first sight
- baby blue
- beyond a shadow of a doubt
- bird's eye view

- canary yellow
- catch a glimpse of
- clear cut
- crystal clear
- dim view
- eagle eye
- eye to eye
- field of view
- flashed on
- get a perspective on
- get a scope of
- get the picture
- hazy idea
- horse of a different colour
- in light of
- in the dark
- in the green
- in the pink
- in view of
- make a scene
- mental image
- mental picture
- mind's eye
- naked eye
- paint a picture
- paint the town red
- photographic memory
- picture this
- plainly seen
- point of view
- pretty as a picture
- royal purple
- see at a glance
- see to it
- see you around
- seeing red
- short-sighted
- showing off
- sight for sore eyes
- staring off into space
- take a gander at
- take a peek
- that's clear to me
- the long view
- tunnel vision
- wall-eyes
- well defined

In Business

When you want to present a product, proposal, or point of view to the visual communicator, for optimum understanding and consideration, speak quickly with an excited tone. Using their visual language also assists these individuals in forming a picture and therefore being more willing to envision what you are saying. For example:

- "*Imagine* yourself *clearly* having this [product/service] in the future; what *insight* does this give you about the benefit or value of this purchase?"
- "Can you *see* the [potential benefit or value]? Having that *picture*, you would want to take the time to *view* the brochure, wouldn't you?"
- "If this *looks good* to you, we could go ahead and *focus* on getting the paperwork done."

Personal Interactions

In personal interactions with people with visual in the communication zone, it's helpful to paint a picture with your words. Using visual words also helps them to make a picture of what you are saying:

- "Let's see when we can get together. What date looks best to you?"
- "Could you see us getting together on Sunday for dinner?"

Important Question

As touched upon earlier, the person with visual in the communication zone is absolutely concerned with time. The most important questions for this personality style are *when* questions. They always want to know the timing of things:

- When would you like to meet again?
- When is the deadline?
- When will that be complete?
- When is that available?
- When is that due?
- When can we arrange that?
- When are we getting together again?
- When will it start?
- When will it end?

The *when* questions allow these individuals to get things organized in their timeline so they can make plans. Remember, visual communicators are planners. They are also extremely quick to respond to any question asked of them. They expect others to be the same and can become impatient with those who aren't.

Learning

People with visual in the communication zone grasp concepts quickly. They are intellectual and perceptive, and learning is often fun for them. They enjoy visual stimulation and can easily get bored without it. However, they do not like to deal with too much detail.

They are less distracted by noise than others but can be distracted by movement or anything they can see going on in the environment. Don't try to talk to people with visual in the communication zone while the TV is on or while someone is doing something that catches their attention. They learn best in a situation where there is minimal visual distraction.

Visual communicators learn by seeing. They can memorize by seeing or creating pictures. Of all the personality styles, people with visual in the communication zone are the fastest at processing information because they only need enough detail to form a picture; once they see that picture, they have it. They pick up concepts quickly and, because of that, can get impatient when others need more information or time.

As we would expect, visual learners enjoy and benefit from visual aids, such as pictures, illustrations, written instructions, agendas, demonstrations, and models. When they read information, they create an internal picture or movie which they can easily recall when needed. Some visual learners have the natural ability of photographic memory. They memorize by seeing pictures or the written word. They can see things just once and retrieve that information like a photograph, instantaneously.

Quite often, verbal instructions are not entirely heard by people with visual in the communication zone because their mind tends to wander. They can go off on their own movie of what they think you are going to say after hearing only the first few words uttered. They often have trouble remembering verbal instructions because of this.

For example, if you verbally ask the person with visual in the communication zone to pick up milk, bread, and butter at the store, they may come back with milk only. But if you write the three items down and *show* them the list, even if they don't take the list along, they will remember everything, because they *saw* it.

Major Personality Challenges

The main challenge of individuals with visual in the communication zone is flexibility. They are challenged when plans change at the last minute, because it takes them time to formulate a new picture. Consequently, they can at times appear to be rigid and stubborn.

Perfectionism is another big one for people with visual in the communication zone. They often have high expectations of themselves and others and can be extremely disappointed if the expectations are not met. Because they have such high standards, they generally do very well. Yet perfectionism can be a double-edged sword, as perfectionists may be critical and judgemental of both themselves and others. As mentioned earlier, their thinking can be black and white, and they often assume that the only right way of doing something is their way.

It can be difficult for the person with visual in the communication zone to picture another way of doing something—or if what has been done is of a far different standard than is okay with them. They may not be able to accept it, even if it is something they must live with.

Career/Organizations

People with visual in the communication zone are known for their high standards for impeccability at work. They are the visionaries, and they want their own work—and that of those they work with—to be the best possible. They want everything to run flawlessly and smoothly. They not only grasp the big picture quickly, they also comprehend all of the facets of the project and even pick up on details others miss.

Visual people are generally organized, neat, and tidy in their work environment, and they expect this in others. They need to be organized, with their priorities in place, so that they can stay on track and not get overwhelmed by the tasks at hand. They often prefer to do business in person, especially at first, so they can see the person they are dealing with and that person's responses.

If they have the opportunity to form an overall picture, they can plan and organize projects and events second to none. Because of their ability to visualize, they have the incredible talent of being able to see in their mind's eye the completed project in detail—to know exactly what it will look like. Because they carry this vision clearly in their mind, they have the ability to present the plan and to guide others in it.

Getting recognized and acknowledged for their work is important. Praise, appreciation, and recognition—given in a visible way—will keep them motivated to do their best. On the other hand, if they are not given visible recognition, it can lead to dissatisfaction.

Bosses with visual in the communication zone can be exacting, as they feel that everything done by the people under their jurisdiction reflects on them. Part of the reason for their perfectionistic attitude is their need to do things right the first time. This can keep them from attempting new things that require a steep learning curve, as they may be afraid of looking foolish or ill-prepared.

They can be team players or leaders as long as they can see their part in the project or job and have enough influence to effectively guide others. Being organized helps them to delegate well. Sometimes, however, they have difficulty working with a team if they have a different picture or vision of what the project is. They often like to work alone because they can do it their way and don't have to deal with different standards than their own.

If a person with visual in the communication zone asks if this or that can be done and you aren't sure, clearly say, "I don't know." If you answer *yes*, *maybe*, or *we'll see*, it will take time and some disappointment on their part to change their picture if needed.

Amusement and Humour

As intellectuals, people with visual in the communication zone can be wickedly sarcastic in their humour and often are. Of course, they particularly like visually rich forms of recreation and entertainment, as seeing it is what is important to them. Examples include live music concerts, theatre, or ballet; beautiful scenes or places; optical illusions; cartoons; or anything they see that looks intriguing or funny to them in a movie, TV, or life.

Regarding humour, they really dislike being made to look foolish or silly. If this happens, it can take quite a long time for them to get past it or forgive it, if they ever do.

Decisions

People with visual in the communication zone will make conclusions and decisions based on what they have seen or been shown—and on how it appears or looks to them. Once they have the picture, they are very quick to make decisions. Seeing is believing, and once these individuals have made a decision and pictured it, unless you can change that picture, it will be hard to get them to change their minds.

Physical Space

Ambience and beautiful things are almost as important as breathing to visual communicators. Yes, it is important to them that their environment be well organized, but more than that, they love beautiful things—pictures, art, plants, architecture, and natural light. They have a great ability with visual and spatial perception and can understand the relationship between space and effect.

If the physical environment is inharmonious or totally disorganized, this will put people with visual in the communication zone into discord, and they won't be able to function well.

Physiology

Breathing

People with visual in the communication zone tend to breathe from the top of their lungs, often in shallow, quick breaths. Sometimes, if they are talking quickly, you can hardly see them breathe. When they are talking quickly and excitedly, they will do skip breathing—tiny, almost undetectable breaths snuck in between words.

Movement

Generally, their movements are faster than those of people with other communication styles. When they are not moving, they can be utterly still and focused. They can gaze off into space and sit very still while watching an internal movie, sometimes for long periods of time. When visual communicators are moving, though, they are generally quick and precise in their movements and get things done in short order.

Gestures

Their gestures are often grand, extending up above their shoulders. They seem to be saying with their gestures, "Look up and see the bigger picture"—the movie, the panorama, the dream, the vision. Usually, the person with visual in the communication zone will use gestures for effect, to make a point, or to paint the picture in front of you.

Physicality

Visual communicators are completely aware of how they look and how what they are doing looks. They will do things to look "good" and avoid things that may make them look "bad," according to their standards. They will often stand or sit with their heads and/or bodies more erect and look up with their eyes often, looking for pictures they have formed internally.

Sometimes, if they are running an internal movie, they may look at a particular spot out in front of them. They tend to sit forward in their chair and like to have enough distance between them and the other person that they can see that individual clearly and get the whole picture. They want to see what is going on and what you are talking about, and they will do what is physically necessary to do that—such as move or change positions/seats.

When upset, visual communicators can appear to be giving you "the look." But the real reason for this kind of expression may be that they are upset with themselves or are having an internal moment.

Out-of-Balance Tendencies

When people with visual in the communication zone go out of balance, they can become extremely stubborn and rigid. They get totally stuck in whatever picture/movie they have and seem totally inflexible. They can also become quite critical and judgemental. They will quickly spot errors in other people's work or ideas and think it's their duty to correct them.

The drive for perfection makes these individuals their own worst enemy, because they are so critical of themselves they can't take even the slightest criticism from someone else. They may interpret a simple difference of opinion as a criticism or an attempt to put them down. In their out-of-balance state, nothing seems to be meeting their expectations, and they can take a disappointed and tragic view of life. They may even run themselves into a tired and confused state by giving compulsively focused attention to negative emotional memories in the form of pictures. They can become discouraged and disillusioned and may even give up.

At such times, people with visual in the communication zone can withdraw into themselves, become extremely demanding, and over-exaggerate their emotional needs, making them unable to handle any pressure. Their tendency toward black-and-white thinking can become much more pronounced. Until they come into a more balanced state, they tend to feel that their way of doing things is the only "right way"—they cannot conceive of any other way being valid If they lack self-awareness, they can become anxious, worry a lot about little things, get stuck in the small picture, and become easily upset at almost anything.

In order to try to escape themselves, they can become emotionally involved in other people's problems (when out of balance, they get a sense of control when others ask them for advice or depend on them). Out-of-balance people with visual in the communication zone have a tendency to either not hear what others are telling them or to hear very selectively. This, of course, results in many misunderstandings. Also, timing becomes an even bigger issue than usual: they want everyone to move in their timing, and they get impatient when that doesn't happen. This adds stress to their relationships.

These individuals are so hyper-aware of how things look that they will straighten pictures in other people's homes, or tell them if their slip is showing, or feel compelled to leave if the environment is too disorganized or out of harmony. To bring themselves back into balance, they need to visualize and reconnect with the bigger picture, and they need to clean up, get organized, and set a plan of action. It helps them a great deal to have something to work towards and look forward to. Sometimes they need to have a timeout or a mini-vacation.

Review of Visual in the Communication Zone

Highest Values

- beauty, ambience, that which is visually pleasing
- balance
- harmony

Needs

- to be organized
- to have a plan
- to have their priorities set
- to have something to look forward to
- to have an attractive, pleasant environment
- to move in their own timing
- to be in balance (visually, time-wise, in life)

Challenges

- fixed pictures
- inflexibility
- perfectionism
- criticalness
- worry/anxiety
- attachment to timing and scheduling
- can put other people under time pressure

How Others Describe Them

- critical
- friendly
- impatient
- inflexible
- intellectual
- intelligent
- judgemental
- list people
- orderly
- organized
- patient
- peaceful
- perfectionist
- planner
- promoter
- pushy
- sarcastic
- selfish
- serious
- soft-hearted
- stubborn
- visionary

- warm
- well integrated

Out-of-Balance Behaviours

- being rigid
- lacking flexibility
- getting stuck in fixed pictures
- placing time pressure on self and others
- acting critical and judgemental
- getting stuck in black-and-white thinking
- feeling duty-bound to point out and correct others' mistakes
- insisting there's only one right way
- being unable to handle pressure
- over-exaggerating emotional needs
- worrying a lot
- focusing on old pictures of emotionally negative experiences
- getting stuck in the small picture

Solutions to Create Balance

- See the bigger picture.
- Clean up.
- Get organized.
- Set priorities.
- Put together a plan of action.
- Have something to look forward to.
- Work towards goals.
- Take time out for a mini-vacation.

Chapter 10
The Communication Zone: Cognitive

Unique Characteristics Overview

People with cognitive in the communication zone are constantly making meaning and sense out of the world around them and continually jumping to conclusions about things. They have a strong concern for the future. Because they are future-oriented, they often think of ideas or create plans that are ahead of their time.

Out of all the communication zones, people with cognitive in the communication zone are the ones who process internally the most. This means that they think things through in their head thoroughly—they gather information, internalize, analyse, sequence, find meaning, draw conclusions, and make assumptions—and only then feel ready to share their conclusions with others.

People with cognitive in the communication zone talk in conclusions or questions, which gives them an air of authority. You can identify them by their frequent use of the phrases "I know" or "That makes sense." They just know things, although they often don't know how they know them. It's as if they have a sixth sense. They have this natural wisdom that gives them knowledge without being told. They have strong hunches, intuition, and sometimes even premonitions.

Their highest value is integrity, and their word is their bond. This can be taken to extremes at times, and they will go way beyond what is normally expected in order to do what they have promised. They are extremely independent and strive for and encourage self-sufficiency. A common theme with people with cognitive in the communication zone is that they are always looking to improve themselves, their designs, ideas, plans, life, and everything they are interested in.

They inherently have a keen insight into people and situations and are responsive to the ideas and feelings of others. They respect others and realize that all persons must discover their own path. When they are in balance, they can easily assist others without involving their own ego.

Through their inner awareness, people with cognitive in the communication zone often sense others' potential and what they can become. These individuals get great satisfaction from assisting others to develop that potential. When they are motivated to help others, they feel hurt if someone takes offense at their encouragement to improve, which only stems from a deep caring. They usually have a strong awareness of their own feelings and motivation. They have an absolute need for personal freedom in their lives and so recognize the importance of personal freedom for others.

They are extensively logically minded. Everything has a sequence and an order to it. It could be dates—like January 21, this happened; then February 20, this happened; then, March 18, this happened—or numbers—first this, second that, or 1, 2, 3, or even letters, like A, B, C.

These individuals are great at detecting patterns, reasoning, analysing problems, and coming up with solutions. They maintain a necessary sense of security through a sense of order, personal control, and personal direction. Having a secure home base is critical for them, as it allows them to be solid in their personal world, which in turn allows them to be out in the external world with confidence. This could mean owning their own home, having a secure foundation in their relationship, or if on holiday, having a hotel room to do excursions from—whatever a secure home base means to them.

They love information, ask a lot of questions, and seem to absorb information like a sponge. They will show their interest in a person or topic by asking questions. But if they decide they aren't interested, they'll ignore that person or change the subject.

They are extremely compartmentalized in their lives. Work is work, home is home, social is social, and each may have several compartments. Their spouse/partner and children may even have their own compartments. Everything is broken down into categories. For example, they may have a friend they play tennis with, another they play cards with, and yet another they meet for lunch regularly. Each friend would have a specific compartment; they might never meet each other.

Quite often, if something has been placed in one compartment, it will not overlap with another. Since they are the only ones with a communication zone component that is compartmentalized in this way, when they look to how others conduct their affairs, it can seem to them as if those people's lives are all enmeshed and lacking order and structure. They are notably singularly focused and have a high degree of concentration. When they are in one sequence or compartment, the others are not in their focus, and this sometimes leads people to accuse them of being absent-minded.

They want to be in the know about everything that involves them or interests them, including their relationships. They don't necessarily need to do anything with the information; it just helps them to make sense of and be comfortable in their world. However, although they like information, they don't often volunteer much about themselves or what they are doing unless asked specific questions. Even then, it depends on who is asking as to whether or not they will give out the information.

Often, people with cognitive in the communication zone will gather information, analyse it, come to conclusions, and make a decision, because that sequence is finished for them—they do this all without even thinking to share that information with others, even the people they are closest to.

Once people with cognitive in the communication zone know something, they have a tendency to think everyone knows it and are often surprised when others reveal that they don't. For example, consider a person with cognitive in the communication zone at work in a meeting with the management team, which is looking for a solution. This person states what seems to be the obvious answer, and then everyone responds with, "Wow, that's a great idea! How did you come up with that?" Because of the way these people process, what is obvious to them is not obvious to others, and they are often surprised by this.

They are significantly private people and have a tendency to make a few very deep, loyal friendships. They tend to put people they know into other categories, such as workmate, tennis partner, member of the choir, or acquaintance. People with cognitive in the communication zone will spend a fair amount of time talking to themselves, either internally or out loud. This is one of their ways of creating order and organizing things. Often they think some of their best conversations are with themselves!

People with cognitive in the communication zone command respect just by their natural way of being in the world. They have an air of authority about them that most often they are unaware of. They are surprised to find out it exists.

When people with cognitive in the communication zone come into a new situation or are around people they haven't met before, they are quite often thought to be shy, reserved, or standoffish. But that is untrue. They are actually observing, gathering information, and casing the situation or people. They are working to make sense out of where they fit, what or who they are interested in, and what part they want to play, if any. Once they have figured it out, their behaviour can range from gregarious to silent or anywhere in between, depending on their conclusions.

They are often thought of as extroverts but are actually introverts who have the ability to be extroverted at times. *Rebel* is the word which best describes people with cognitive in the communication zone, for they can be downright rebellious, particularly if they don't understand the purpose of a directive or feel they are not being given a choice. But they can be cooperative if the reasons for guidelines or rules make sense and if they agree.

Choice and freedom are extremely high values for the person with cognitive in the communication zone. They generally do not follow the beaten track or the crowd. They like to be unique and are often described as being a little different or a bit eccentric—a description which they actually appreciate.

People with cognitive in the communication zone need to be creative, though not necessarily in the traditional sense. They enjoy being creative with all that they do. They enjoy creatively putting a program together, creatively organizing an event, creatively writing up a proposal, and creatively putting a system together. If they have no opportunity to be creative, they will be very moody or even depressed.

Most often, the person with cognitive in the communication zone is a night owl, getting into projects or entertainment late in the evening and into the wee hours of the morning. These individuals are generally not morning people, but they can be when necessity calls or if they decide and train themselves to be.

Trust is a challenge for the person with cognitive in the communication zone. Either they are too trusting (believing the words addressed to them) or not trusting enough (questioning everything). If they don't have a sense of control over their own life, they can become quite controlling of everyone and everything around them. For example: Jeremy got fired from his job and feels out of control, so he starts to try to control everything going on in his household and everyone in the house. He may not even know he is doing this; he is just trying to get a sense of control over his own life.

These individuals can have a tendency to isolate themselves while they are working through something internally. But once they have made sense out of the issue or have made their conclusion, they will come out of isolation.

People with cognitive in the communication zone want others when they want them—and don't want others when they don't want them. They can be fully people-oriented and yet need their alone time or downtime to process. As rebooting is a computer's chance to clean itself up, so is downtime and alone time to the person with cognitive in the communication zone. When they don't get this, they can become irritable and out-of-balance, and they seek escapism in many forms (excessive eating, TV watching, computer games, alcohol, porn, etc.)

They are totally sensual people and like good food, good sex, and good sleep, though not necessarily in that order. They have an exceptionally keen sense of smell and taste and appreciate the sensual things in life. They have an interesting relationship with food and eating. If they have not scheduled eating into their plans and they are working on a project, they will often not stop until they have finished the project or at least a major part of it. Then they will want to eat right now—not five minutes from now, but right now.

Sometimes they go beyond the point of feeling their hunger and go into a state similar to hyperglycaemia in which they can't make a decision. Recently, this has been termed *hangry*. In this condition, they can't take the slightest amount of pressure without being grumpy or abrupt. They do not usually know that they are in this state, but everyone around them will notice that they are not themselves. However, as soon as they eat, they become normal again. Therefore, it is absolutely important for the person with cognitive in the communication zone to schedule in regular eating times, as this actually helps the individual to be more productive, make better decisions, and be a whole lot more fun to be around.

Because of their creative and sensual nature, of all the communication zones, those with cognitive in the communication zone have the highest sex drive. They enjoy sexual innuendo and flirtation, male or female. This has nothing to do with gender. They like to play with sexual energy, and they see it as an entirely natural and wonderful part of life. A good sexual relationship with their partner makes them feel deeply loved, and they like to show their love to their partner through good sexual relations, flirtation, and sexual innuendo.

The fact that other communication zones are different in this area can sometimes lead to misunderstandings. For example, a flirtatious remark or off-coloured joke meant to be funny might be made inappropriately.

Communication

Words, words, words. Words are of the utmost importance to the person with cognitive in the communication zone. Most of the people with other components in the communication zone will take a look at the whole sentence and give it meaning, but the person with cognitive in the communication zone looks at each word in the sentence and gives each word meaning before giving the sentence meaning. If one word does not fit for these individuals or they do not know or like the meaning that you are using, they will get stuck on that word and may even argue about it.

The interpretation and explanation of ideas and information through language—written or spoken—is a critical foundation upon which communication is based. Argument, debate, discussion, and questioning are natural ways for people with cognitive in the communication zone to make sense of their world. They are articulate and diplomatic and able to describe things from many perspectives. In their personal expression, they are usually direct, accurate, and dependable.

These individuals communicate using a range of language and physiology, and they do it in a reasonable, logical fashion. They will often include more data, dates, and numbers in their language than the other processing styles. Because they tend to think before they speak, they need time to formulate their replies.

Depending on the situation, they are generally good listeners. They can at times interrupt people because in their mind, they have finished what the other person is saying. They can be impatient to share their thoughts on a subject and can enjoy asking questions. When they are impassioned about something or excited to share, they may be totally unaware that they are even interrupting.

People with cognitive in the communication zone can get so much into their own heads that they can be quite stunned when accused of being reserved, arrogant, aloof, and/or argumentative. At times, they are captivating speakers; at other times, they bore or overwhelm listeners with too much data. They love discussions on topics that interest them and can argue both sides of an issue just for fun. They also do this to gather different ideas and perspectives. They do enjoy a good debate.

Because people with cognitive in the communication zone thinks things through before saying anything, they say what they mean and mean what they say. Since they naturally talk in conclusions, their words carry the ring of authority. Other processing styles can misinterpret their intent and may even say they talk "as if God has spoken" because it sounds as if the cognitive communicator is making a decree. Even when these individuals seek input, others can get the impression that they have already made up their mind. They often forget to ask for input, but that doesn't mean they don't care, as they willingly give their opinions without being asked and expect that others will do this as easily as they do.

People with cognitive in the communication zone want to be in the know in every area that they feel pertains to them, and so they will often ask questions to get whatever information they need to make sense of the situation. Often these questions are *what* questions, such as the following:

- "What are you up to?"
- "What is the objective?"
- "What are we going to do next?"
- "What is that?"

Words are everything to the person with cognitive in the communication zone, and they will often give more weight to what a person has said than to other things that are going on. They believe that their word is their bond and expect others to abide by that same code of behaviour. Because they are extremely particular about the words they use, they expect that others will be also and get confused and sometimes even upset when they find otherwise.

People with cognitive in the communication zone are information people, and they will often listen silently and intently to others and not participate in a conversation unless directly asked a question. They also enjoy a good debate or argument if they get more understanding or a larger perspective. Since words are their thing, they are naturally good storytellers when they choose to be, and—as you might expect—enjoy using language or metaphor to get a point across.

Language

Speech Patterns

People with cognitive in the communication zone can exhibit characteristics and language of all the communication zones. What sets them apart is that everything will have a sequence and order to it. They will spend a fair amount of time talking to themselves (either inside their head or out loud to themselves). They use deliberate phrasing, speak in conclusions, and are logical.

They tend to take things said or written literally. They will not give an indication of understanding unless you ask them. They often say "I know" a lot. All dates, numbers, and data are considered to be cognitive, and these individuals will naturally use them. Everything having to do with mental processes is considered cognitive, and people with cognitive in the communication zone actively uses these things in their speech. Typical words and phrases include the following:

Mental processing words
- analyse
- assumption
- awareness
- believe
- comprehend
- conceive
- concentration
- conclusion
- consider
- contemplate
- decide
- deduce
- digital
- enlightenment
- experience
- faith
- imagine
- integrity
- judgement
- know
- learn
- meaning
- meditate
- muse
- perceive
- presume
- principle
- process
- question
- realize
- reason
- recall
- reflect
- remember
- sense
- sequence
- surmise
- think
- trust
- understand
- wonder

Other cognitive words
- advice
- advise
- change
- communicate
- concept
- conscious
- conviction
- data
- declaration
- deliberate
- distinct
- educate
- exaggerate
- honesty
- idea
- infer
- information
- instruct
- intercourse
- justification
- knowledge
- language
- mediate
- message
- mind
- motivate
- opinion
- persuasion
- possible
- probable
- procedure
- rational
- report
- sequence
- teach
- unconscious
- words

All dates
- January
- February
- March
- April
- May
- June
- July
- August
- September
- October
- November
- December

All numbers or sequencing
- using either digits, 1, 2, 3; or letters, A, B, C
- also numbers spelled out, like *first, second*, etc.

All data
- facts and statistics collected together for reference, analysis, or calculations

Phrases
- a sense of ...
- be conscious of
- change is good
- consider learning ...
- considering that ...
- distinct possibility of ...
- Does that make sense?
- I can conceive of that.
- I can experience ...
- I don't know ...
- I don't understand your meaning.
- I have a real knowing about that.
- I know.
- I need more information.
- I perceive that to be ...
- I sense that ...
- I thought ...
- I understand that ...
- I will consider your question.
- I wonder if ...
- in that process
- inquire into
- make a decision
- make sense
- my discernment
- my idea
- reason it through
- That makes sense.
- That's a good question.
- the conscious conception is ...
- the content included ...
- the learning process ...
- the procedures are ...
- the process is ...
- the wonder of it all
- the word on that is ...
- thinking about that
- to motivate, you can ...
- to sequence it
- understanding is ...
- without a doubt
- word for word
- You know what I mean.

In Business

When you want the cognitive person to consider your product, proposal, or point of view, for optimum understanding and consideration, use a thoughtful and considerate tone of voice. A logical sequence and order to your presentation and the use of cognitive language also helps. When you use their language, it helps cognitive communicators make sense of what you are saying, which in turn helps them make a conclusion. For example:

- "If I could give you the *information* and *statistics* that can assist you in *knowing how this* may benefit you, you would at least want to *consider* it, wouldn't you?"
- "If this makes *sense* to you, we will go ahead and set it up by *processing* the paperwork."

Personal Interactions

In personal interactions with people with cognitive in the communication zone, it's helpful to use a logical sequence and use cognitive words that assist them in processing and making sense of the question or information:
- "Could you think about a good *time* to get together?"
- "Do you know what a good *time* to get together would be?"

Important Question

The most important questions for the person with cognitive in the communication zone are *what* questions:

- What's happening?
- What's going on?
- What are we going to do about that?
- What's your opinion?
- What's that about?
- What do you want to do?
- What have we covered so far?
- What is left to do?
- What are the facts?
- What are you doing?
- What have you heard?
- What's the word on that?

They want information so they can make sense of it. They are natural information-gatherers constantly analysing themselves and the world. People with cognitive in the communication zone want data so they can understand or know where it fits.

Learning

People with cognitive in the communication zone tend to think out loud. Consequently, they often talk to themselves. This self-talk is one of their ways of organizing and sequencing things. They find future possibilities intriguing and can get bored by the present. They are often more interested in where things are going than where matters stand in the present. They sometimes need reminding to be present, as they have a tendency to be too focused on the future.

They memorize, learn, and operate in the world by steps, procedures, and sequences. They will want to know if something "makes sense."

People with cognitive in the communication zone spontaneously go in and out of a kind of light trance during the process of learning. They are sometimes accused of daydreaming, but when asked what was being said, they will often be able to repeat it back word for word. This trance occurs because they are constantly going from gathering information in the outside world to fitting it in and making sense of it according to what they already know in their internal world. They may be re-evaluating or expanding on what is already known. In order to understand an event or communication, they must make reasonable logical sense of it and give it meaning.

Cognitive communicators will often work problems through in their sleep. They have been known to dream a lot—even dream and work out an entire paper or project during their slumber. Einstein was known for taking a nap whenever he hit an impasse; he would ask himself questions, take a nap, and wake up with the answers. Einstein most likely had cognitive in his communication zone.

Those with cognitive in the communication zone have an incredible ability to cross-reference material from one area to another—they naturally take all information to the abstract to see where it makes sense or fits, and they can then apply that to a given topic or topics. For example, they may be listening to all of the conversation and data being spoken about at the meeting they are attending, and while they are doing that, they remember information they heard a year ago about a totally different project. When they automatically take it out to the abstract, they conceive of a way of combining that information that will solve or assist in the problem that is being discussed.

Once people with cognitive in the communication zone have made a conclusion about something, they will continue to believe the conclusion is right, until or unless they receive enough logical reasonable information to require them to re-evaluate. These individuals can at times have trouble admitting they don't know something and can put extreme or unrealistic pressure on themselves to know things. They think they should already know things. This is particularly true of children and teenagers with cognitive in the communication zone. They can put themselves under unnecessary pressure because they have not yet learned that it is okay to not know something.

Although they love information, people with cognitive in the communication zone do not like education for education's sake. They need their studies to be of value to them, or at least of interest, and to fit in with their life's plan. Otherwise, they will do just enough to get by.

Major Personality Challenges

Trust is the major challenge for those with cognitive in the communication zone. These individuals are either too trusting—taking people at their word without question and assuming what others say is exactly what they mean or will do—or not trusting enough—being sceptical and questioning everything. More often than not, the person with cognitive in the communication zone has difficulty taking things at face value. Superficial knowledge is just not enough. Cognitive communicators are known for being sceptics and for wanting *all* the information.

Another challenge is that people with cognitive in the communication zone don't just *like* to be right about things; they *love* it. Just as much, they hate being wrong—although they will re-evaluate if you give them enough logical, reasonable information.

These individuals need to have closure and can be relentless until they get it. This applies to most things and particularly to emotional issues; they will be extremely persistent in getting closure even when that may not always be what's best. For example, I knew of a couple who, when they had a disagreement, would follow this pattern: They would be arguing, and the intensity would go up. The one who was kinesthetic in her communication zone would decide they were done with the communication; sometimes she would say that, but often she would not say anything but would just leave, go into the bathroom, and lock the door. The person who was cognitive in his communication zone would then go to the bathroom door and continue to argue through the door. You can see how this would not be in either one's best interest.

Those with cognitive in the communication zone also have a tendency to take on more projects than they can effectively handle and spread themselves too thin. They need to learn how to prioritize.

Career/Organizations

People with cognitive in the communication zone plan ahead and can carry extensive projects through to completion. They command respect and are productive. People with cognitive in the communication zone usually grasp the overall picture—including all the important details—quickly. They need to be in the bigger, longer-term picture and think too many details are boring and redundant.

These individuals have more than their fair share of common sense. They may actually have developed the whole concept around common sense, since common sense is not really common! They have the remarkable ability to be focused on what they are doing and at the same time think about other things. They have brains somewhat like computers in that they can be completely focused and absorbed by the task at hand but in the background, their brains are computing other issues. When they stop the task or later when they are relaxing, often they just know things or have worked out a solution for something else.

With their ability to quickly size up and weigh situations, they excel as executives and/or in areas of management. People with cognitive in the communication zone work well with all processing styles and have innate skills when it comes to managing people and projects. Diplomacy is the middle name of people with cognitive in the communication zone. Because they have such a gift with words, they generally handle people and events with utmost tact.

Words and the skilful usage of words, both written and spoken, come easily to people with cognitive in the communication zone. They can talk themselves in or out of almost any situation. They can justify just about anything when they put their mind to it, and their use of language, reason, and logic can be completely convincing.

People with cognitive in the communication zone are totally compartmentalized in their mind and their life, and therefore, when they are in one compartment, they are not in another. This allows them to have a sense of control. It is extremely important that people with cognitive in the communication zone have a sense of control over their own lives. They dislike being controlled or being told what to do. So, some autonomy on the job makes a better fit for them.

They love having choices and often have difficulty with authority figures because they view everyone as equal and need the reasoning and logic behind whatever is being asked of them. They must respect a person and believe that person knows what he or she is doing to take direction from that person. If they don't respect the person or believe that the person lacks knowledge, individuals with cognitive in the communication zone will have trouble working with them.

Importantly, they have an innate ability to find and seek the connections, the interrelatedness behind things. This helps them to give or find meaning. Often, they have difficulty taking things at face value and like figuring out how things work or what makes a person tick for the sheer pleasure of knowing.

They do have a tendency towards ambiguity when answering questions. If they know something, they often assume that everyone else knows it. They can be shocked when others don't see the obvious connections that they find so easily, or they can be impatient when they know things and others don't.

Since integrity is their top value, they have high levels of integrity on the job and in everything they do, and they value this in others. They take a great deal of pride in being fair-minded and gentle-hearted as well as in their reasonableness and objectivity. However, because they can remain level-headed even when others are upset, they can be accused by those who don't understand them of being cold, uncaring, or intimidating, and this can shock them.

They can have an uncanny knack for numbers and figures. They often remember things like phone numbers but may forget a person's name. People with cognitive in the communication zone prefer to work from a schedule as long as it is a flexible one. They like systems, routine, and order.

They can't stand stagnation in a job, relationship, or project. They need to be working towards something, learning something, or being creative. They want life to have meaning and to contribute. They are future-oriented in their approach to all things. If stagnation happens, they can become quite out-of-balance and critical, even depressed, or they may want to leave the situation.

People with cognitive in the communication zone have an incredible capacity for getting a lot done in a fairly short period of time. They generally handle stressful situations well as long as they have learned to prioritize.

Amusement and Humour

People with cognitive in the communication zone usually have a well-developed sense of humour (or think they do) and enjoy their own jokes immensely. They like puns, plays on words, word games, combining words, acronyms, jokes that utilize different meanings for words, sexual jokes (overt or implied), innuendo, political jokes, and jokes that make people think. ("Well, I once heard a story of the past, the present, and the future walking into a bar. I am sad to say that it was tense.")

They also like information on any topic they are interested in, and good books, documentaries, and movies. They enjoy discussion, conversation, and debate.

Decisions

Those with cognitive in the communication zone are usually good at decision-making. When they know inside that the decision is right, they will take action. They can naturally take a lot of information, analyse it, make sense of it, and reduce and condense it to a couple of conclusions. Often when they share their conclusions about things with others, it can have an impact on those around them. This is why people naturally respect them.

When making decisions, people with cognitive in the communication zone will gather information and think it through until they can make a logical, reasonable choice. Because information is key for them, often they want all the data before making the decision: facts, percentages, statistics, comparative reports, and so on.

Physical Space

In their physical space, people with cognitive in the communication zone will usually want order. Everything has a place and an order to it. It must be functional with convenience of movement.

The way in which these individuals interact with their home space or office space will often have a routine or schedule. Sometimes it is a very flexible one, and at other times it is more rigid. They will even apply a sequence and order to their environment outside of their home and office.

For example, when people with cognitive in the communication zone are travelling and doing errands, they will plan their route, if possible, so they don't have to backtrack at any point. They will want to go to the gas station that is on the side of the road they are driving on, etc. This, they will tell you, is just common sense.

Physiology

People with cognitive in the communication zone can exhibit characteristics of all the other communication styles. Their breathing and gestures move in a range of all the others. These people will spend a fair amount of time talking to themselves. They will want to know if what you are talking about "makes sense."

People with cognitive in the communication zone think in a more digital way, which means that the words themselves, theoretically, are discrete units of meaning. For example, consider the difference between an analogue clock and a digital clock. An analogue clock has a hand (or a marker) that moves through the full spectrum. So analogue means that the full range has meaning, whereas the digital clock is totally specific or precise and each second has meaning.

People with cognitive in the communication zone therefore think more digitally because each word in a sentence has a specific meaning for them, before the entire sentence can have meaning. In NLP, this part of the brain is referred to as *digital* (or auditory digital) for that reason.

Although not technically their physiology, what makes the person with cognitive in the communication zone stand apart is their attention to the sequencing of things. They will always follow the datelines of things occurring or the steps, one by one. Or they will throw in things like data, names, dates, financial figures, numbers, percentages, and statistics. But generally, their utilization of other communication styles, language, and physiology allows them to relate easily to most processing styles.

Breathing

They utilizes a wide range, from high to low and everywhere in between.

Movement

People with cognitive in the communication zone move from total stillness to total movement as needed to get the point across or to demonstrate what they want to demonstrate.

Gestures

These individuals utilize a range from above the shoulders to below the waist and all areas in between.

Physicality

A remarkably wide range of physicality, utilizing all of the other components.

Out-of-Balance Tendencies

When people with cognitive in the communication zone go out of balance, procrastination can become a way of life. They may also focus on the negative and how difficult it is to change their bad habits; they may even get caught up in talking to themselves about it in their head. It is important for the person with cognitive in the communication zone to learn to focus on constructive thoughts and reject negative ones.

Often, when out of balance, these individuals can go inside and stay there, becoming isolated and spending more and more time on their own. Too much isolation is not good for the person with cognitive in the communication zone. As much as they need to have appropriate alone time, they also need to be around people. Balancing those two things is a necessity.

People with cognitive in the communication zone can become aloof, arrogant, or know-it-all depending on how out-of-balance they are. They can also become controlling. If they are feeling out of control of their own life, they may want to control everything and everyone around them.

Appearances can be deceiving. When out of balance, people with cognitive in the communication zone can at times appear to be overconfident or superior, though they are actually upset or insecure. They have the ability to not react emotionally and can come across as calculating, uncaring, or disinterested.

If they're not being creative in their lives, they can be flat-out moody, hard to get along with, and closed-down. Having something creative is a need for people with cognitive in the communication zone.

Because people with cognitive in the communication zone can usually handle more on their plate in terms of projects than other processing styles, they can have a tendency to take on more than they can effectively handle. Out of balance and sometimes even in balance, they can overwhelm themselves with too many projects and need to learn to prioritize and sort which projects are important.

One of the most destructive behaviours when out of balance for the person with cognitive in the communication zone is a tendency towards escapist behaviour. When really out of balance, these individuals have a tendency to be self-destructive. They may take things to extremes, becoming addicted to alcohol, drugs, sex, porn, food, gambling, shopping, or even things like computers, reading, TV, or golf. Most of these activities are fine in moderation; it's only when those with cognitive in the communication zone go out of balance and try to escape their own mind that this becomes an issue. They need to be aware of this addictive tendency to avoid losing control of their lives.

These individuals can also become interrogators when out of balance, asking a lot of questions or becoming very nosey about other people's business. Those with cognitive in the communication zone are often rebellious, but when they go out of balance, they can get into rebelling just for rebellion's sake and be contrary for no reason at all.

Because they can justify just about anything, when challenged, they can come up with totally convincing answers that are in fact made-up stories. They are known for being the best BS-ers on the planet. When out of balance, because things often come easily to them, they look for things to be more complex and can at times make a big deal out of something, overemphasizing a minor problem or difficulty until they create a real issue—in other words, making a mountain out of a molehill.

They can become quite untrusting and at times even paranoid when out of balance, and they may fear change. When out of balance, they can have a particularly hard time admitting to being wrong, and they may argue the point even beyond when they know they are wrong.

Because they have a good use of language and are deeply intuitive, these individuals can be quite intimidating—and when out of balance in an argument, they seem to know exactly where to hit and how hard. The person with cognitive in the communication zone can quickly pick up on your weakest area and point it out with a vicious tongue. These individuals need to learn to take responsibility for this power and use it wisely, not viciously. Fortunately, all of this changes as people with cognitive in the communication zone brings themselves back into balance.

Review of Cognitive in the Communication Zone

Highest Values

- integrity
- freedom
- choice
- independence

Needs

- to be creative
- to have a future plan
- to make sense of things
- to have order and sequence
- to have alone time (emotional space)
- to have downtime (time to space out, dream, do something mindless)
- to have a sense of control over one's own life
- to be in the know (to know things)
- to gather information
- to ask question
- to discuss things (talk about things of interest, of importance)
- to have time to formulate answers

Challenges

- trust (too trusting or not trusting enough)
- escapism
- jumping to conclusions
- interrupting people
- if not interested, can get sleepy or trance out or ignore
- can come across as authoritarian
- future-oriented, so can find it challenging to be in the here and now

How Others Describe Them

- aloof
- analytical
- argumentative
- arrogant
- authoritarian
- controlling
- data-oriented
- diplomatic
- idealist
- know-it-alls
- logical
- objective
- observer
- permissive
- questioning

- reasonable
- rebels
- reserved
- scientific
- serious
- solution-oriented
- standoffish
- thinkers
- voice of reason

Out-of-Balance Behaviours

- self-isolating
- procrastinating
- controlling
- being a know-it-all
- engaging in escapist behaviour
- rebelling
- intimidating
- needing to be right
- feeling overwhelmed
- feeling self-righteous
- acting moody

Solutions to Create Balance

- Prioritize.
- Make a future plan.
- Create order.
- Create routine.
- Gather missing information
- Create appropriate downtime.
- Balance or create some alone time.
- Be creative or create an outlet for being creative.
- Know it's okay to not know something. (Get comfortable with this).
- Ask yourself empowering questions.
- Focus on positive constructive thoughts and reject negative ones
- Complete unfinished projects.
- Find closure if needed.
- Take time to dream or meditate

Chapter 11
The Communication Zone: Auditory

Unique Characteristics Overview

Adventurers, innovators, and idea people—those with auditory in the communication zone never stop thinking. There's a constant internal dialogue going on in their heads; it actually never stops. They are more original than conventional, and they like lots of variety. They love and think in ideas and can play with ideas just for the fun of it.

They are information people. They love real information (versus theories) and new ways of doing things. They stay tuned into and love all the gadgets and new models of things as they come onto the market.

People with auditory in the communication zone are intense in everything they do, although they may not recognize that they are. They are highly physical, and if these individuals are not physically active in their lives, their intensity will increase and be felt even more by those around them. They actually relax best by doing something physical. They need to burn off excess energy.

They can also balance their intense energy by channelling it into action. But if they don't have an outlet for their energy and also neglect their physical activity, they have a tendency to either explode on others or implode on themselves. Doing nothing is harder and more stressful for them than doing full-on physical activity, like being in a marathon.

Those with auditory in the communication zone are efficient and practical people who are always looking for ways to improve what they are doing. They are born leaders, naturals at spearheading projects, and remarkably accomplishment driven. Often their attitude is, "My way or the highway!" They are extremely direct and to the point in their dealings with other people and also want people to be direct with them. One of their mottos may be, "Lead, follow, or get the hell out of the way."

It is important for them to learn where they stand with others and how to create a bridge from their communication style to other communication styles. This would be beneficial for getting cooperation and respect from others versus creating fear. They have a keen sense of discrimination and acumen, work well with the overall plan or goal, and like challenges. They need to understand things, and they usually grasp concepts quickly.

These individuals often have many projects on the go at one time and are good at multitasking. They need to have a sense of accomplishment daily, because with their intensity of energy, they can go out of balance or get extremely moody very quickly. Their area of difficulty is with people skills and relationships with other communication styles different from their own. They usually want just the facts and tend to be less concerned with what they hear as superficial details.

Fairness is their highest value. They get upset easily if they think they are being treated unfairly. They strive to be fair to others, and they tend to root for the underdog. They are humanitarian, caring individuals who find it easier to look at humanity as a whole than to have many personal, up close, and intimate relationships. Most of the people with auditory in the communication zone have only one or maybe two really close and intimate relationships.

Their partner/spouse, if they have one, is usually their best friend. Auditory communicators show love by sharing ideas—including telling people ways they could improve themselves or their lives. These individuals show they care for you by doing things for you. This usually involves practical things, including gifts with practical uses.

People with auditory in the communication zone tend to only allow touching when they want to be touched and can sometimes see touching as a way of trying to manipulate them. They are extremely private and let very few in. They can have real difficulty knowing what they are actually feeling, as they spend so much time in their head. One might joke, "They are so private that parts of themselves don't even know what they are feeling," and this would have more than a little truth in it!

People with auditory in the communication zone seldom share their feelings even with those close to them and can tend to be self-protective and introspective, sometimes not talking for long periods of time. This can result in an explosive outburst, which can come quickly and often without warning.

They have an abundance of acquaintances from the many different areas of their lives, including job, training, sports teams, clubs, and other areas of interest. They are great networkers—the kind of people who, for example, will set up a friend needing an electrician with an electrician seeking customers. They are independent and will make up their own minds; they are not willing to be overtly influenced by others.

If people with auditory in the communication zone are feeling stressed, they will often feel it in the stomach area. Their emotions get worked out through the physical aspect of living, which is why being physically active is so important for them. They at times process by talking at a person on a specific subject, often over and over repeatedly, until they have come up with a solution to the issue or problem for themselves.

As a general rule, these individuals do not like being told what to do, and particularly resent and will be insulted by being told how to do something. When dealing with people who have auditory in the communication zone, the best strategy is to tell them the end result needed, and they will figure out a way to accomplish the task. Once they have decided to do something, they can be depended upon to get the job done. It won't necessarily be pretty, but it will be functional.

As might be expected, people with auditory in the communication zone like music and sounds around them most of the time. They find that noise can be mood-setting or simply comforting. They can and do like to have background music (often quite loud) or the TV on—or even both at the same time—as they go about their daily life.

When going to sleep or doing a task, these individuals respond strongly to sound. They are soothed by music they like or by background sounds that are rhythmic or constant, like a humidifier or ambient noise. They are irritated by irregular noises or sounds they don't know, like a noisy refrigerator motor that kicks in periodically.

They often have a musical ability and an awareness and appreciation of sound and its uses. They easily recognize tonal and rhythmic patterns and can often tell you what song is playing on the radio after only the first few notes. People with auditory in the communication zone need to understand things. If they can't understand something, they can get frustrated and stuck. When they get stuck, they can just throw the object of frustration aside, giving it no importance, or they can get distracted by the next new thing and ignore it.

Similarly, if they think something is not useful, they will ignore it, throw it out, or not value it, and this can include other people's opinions. As mentioned earlier, people with auditory in the communication zone like the newest gadgets and enjoy exploring the leading edge of anything they are interested in. They are extremely interested in the mechanics of how things work, and as children they probably took things apart in order to understand them.

When buying things, they are more concerned with quality than quantity, and they would rather do without an item of lesser quality until they can afford what they really want. The person with auditory in the communication zone has boundaries and will easily tell you explicitly where they are or at the very least let you know they are not happy with what you have done. They can do this with a look, a tone of voice, or their intensity.

In personal relationships, though, they can be deeply loyal and will stick by their friends.

They are usually good at mathematics and sciences, in part because they like factual information that is simple and compact. They like the challenge of figuring out mysteries and solving problems. They usually have a considerably strong sense of concern for humanity and want to be of service, both in order to help others and to better themselves. People with auditory in the communication zone will give you their opinion on things, asked for or not. They seldom beat around the bush but quite freely and straightforwardly tell you what they think.

Having their financial house in order is absolutely important for people with auditory in the communication zone, for without this in place, they will feel quite insecure and have more of a tendency to be out of balance. Finances often determine their sense of self-worth, and being paid fairly on a job is of great importance to them. They also need to have a definitive direction in life and want to feel a sense of accomplishment and achieve their goals along the way. If they don't feel this, it can put them out of balance. But when auditory communicators are in balance, they are a powerhouse in getting things done.

These individuals have a tendency to be more aware of what's new and on the leading edge than others and are creatively inventive in everything they do. They are information-oriented, but more in terms of what's going on through the five senses and what's objectively real in that moment. You could even say they are the ultimate realists, with an extremely low tolerance for theories they consider irrelevant. Because they are more interested in the real world than in dreaming, they generally find dreaming a waste of time and energy.

They can be completely outgoing and often like to be centre-stage. They lack conformity, like unpredictability, and see the world as a place of endless possibilities. As they like to be on the cutting edge, they can at times be high-rollers and risk-takers. People will often say they are stimulating, interesting, and exciting to be around. However, some processing styles find themselves exhausted by the intensity and constant busyness of the auditory communicator. People with auditory in the communication zone like to stretch and push themselves and those around them, as they feel this shows that they care about people.

Communication

People with auditory in the communication zone are articulate and adept at describing their thoughts and ideas, keeping it factual. They can say a lot in a few words. They have a high need to be heard and so value people who will listen to them. In another way, though, they are sparse with words: when you are communicating with them, once they grasp what you are saying or feel they've heard enough on that topic, they'll change the subject— whether you are done talking or not. When this happens, some processing styles are unclear as to whether they've been understood or not, and this can lead to misunderstandings or communication breakdown.

Paradoxically, those with auditory in the communication zone can be excessively repetitive without knowing it. If you tell them that they have already told you something, they will often say, "No, this is different," and then repeat exactly the same words as before. Although it sounds the same to you, it actually *is* different for them because of what they are doing inside their head with the idea. It is best to realize that they are processing something and just listen without trying to add anything. If you contribute to the conversation, this can actually make the process longer.

Being extremely direct and intense, even blunt at times, in their communications, these individuals can be perceived as aggressive. Often when they are sharing their suggestions, it sounds like they are giving commands. They are unaware of this and are confused when people react negatively to what they are saying. If they think you aren't hearing them, they automatically respond by speaking in a lower tone and getting louder.

People often think they are angry, because when people with auditory in the communication zone are making a point, they emphasize it with intensity and volume. They do this when they are frustrated with what they are doing or with the people who are doing it. They also do this when they are passionate about something. At times, it is hard to tell if they are frustrated or just making a point. Both involve a louder tone.

Although they are generally sparse with their words, people with auditory in the communication zone can be exceptionally talkative. Sometimes it seems like they will never stop talking, while at other times they can be withdrawn and silent, depending on their mood. They process externally by talking at people. Hearing themselves talk out loud helps them to clarify their ideas. They will often blurt things out before the ideas are well formed in order to process the idea by reflecting it off of others. When working things through by talking out loud, they are not really looking for a conversation; they are just looking for someone to bounce their ideas off of because then they can hear themselves work it through. This can be confusing and sometimes even hurtful to those who think they are wanting a conversation.

When people with auditory in the communication zone are talking, they need to finish their sentences because, as mentioned earlier, they are processing as they go. If you interrupt them, they can get frustrated because they need to finish the thought. Even if *you* don't need or want to hear any more, *they* need to hear themselves say it. On the other hand, they interrupt others a lot because others stimulate ideas for them, or they believe they understand what the person is saying and therefore don't need to hear any more. Awareness for the auditory is key here. Recording themselves as they speak about something they are processing is one way auditory communicators can say everything they need to say without interruption and still get to hear themselves say it. Other communication styles can have difficulty understanding what it is these individuals want. People with auditory in the communication zone can have a tendency to use a minimum of words to get the point across, but at other times, when working something out, can give an abundance of detail and appear to love the sound of their own voice. They can use words bluntly and randomly and be quite factual—or be repetitive and go on and on.

When these individuals feel misunderstood or are trying to accomplish something, they can have radically little tolerance for nonfactual information or for other people's different styles of communication. They can display a very low tolerance for what they regard as useless information or communication that they think of as impractical, pointless, or not getting to the point quickly enough.

Because they are blurters who do not think before they speak, they can get themselves into trouble. They don't really listen to themselves the way others do, and if what they said wasn't what they really meant, they delete it from their own minds and even deny having said it in the first place. This can of course create problems when they are asked about it or if someone was offended by what they said. The thing to realize when this happens is that they really don't remember saying it, and no amount of trying to jog their memories will bring it back.

When listening to others speak, because they want the facts and want people to get to the point quickly, they may cut people off and even say things like, "and the point is" or "get to the point." They do not see this as being rude. They are trying to be efficient.

One of the significantly unique things about people with auditory in the communication zone is that they are hypersensitive to other people's tones and volume of voice while being completely oblivious to their own. They can be literally yelling at you or using a sarcastic tone of voice and not know it. Yet if you raise *your* voice even a little or change *your* tone, they will notice and could react negatively towards you.

One of the most important things to people with auditory in the communication zone is being heard. If you interrupt them, appear not to be listening, want to give your own viewpoint, or want to make a suggestion before they are done, they can feel totally insulted. On the other hand, if you paraphrase and give feedback on what they are saying while asking questions that draw out more information, they will feel heard (as long as it is not overdone).

Things have to sound right to the person with auditory in the communication zone, so how it is being said is just as important as the words themselves. If something important is not said with enough intensity, these individuals tend to dismiss it as not important. The people they have the most difficulty with—because they communicate so differently—are those with kinesthetic in the communication zone, who prefer to talk with less intensity and more pauses and soften things so as not to offend anyone.

People with auditory in the communication zone are non-sequential or random thinkers, so they can easily jump from one topic to another or from one part of a topic to another. They don't necessarily talk in a "first this, then that" sequence at all. They may even start at the end and jump to the beginning. This can sometimes lead to confusion for those who are more sequential in their thinking or are trying to get a feeling for what these individuals are talking about. For other styles, it is important to learn how to set boundaries and to firmly tell the auditory communicator that you need a break.

Language

Speech Patterns

Those with auditory in the communication zone often talk in bursts of speech, and if angry, they can use words like a machine gun. When lecturing, they can have a rhythmic or musical quality and tend to use their voice (tone, tempo, and volume) and sound effects to emphasize something or give it life. They will use *uh, um,* and *ah* often as punctuation when speaking. They typically are easily distracted by noise and yet enjoy background noise.

Because hearing is their predominant sense, they don't need to look at you to hear you. They like to talk on the phone, talk to you from another room, or talk to you while they are doing a task. Tone of voice, volume, and the way words are used is important. They can repeat things back to you and learn by listening. They have a rhythmic way of talking and will let you know unconsciously when they understand you by changing the subject.

All sounds, and anything to do with hearing, making, or the quality of sounds, is auditory. This includes speech like "putt-putt-putt" or "the car zoomed by" or "screech around the corner." Typical words and phrases include the following:

Articulating
- aloud
- announce
- answer
- articulation
- assertion
- belittle
- bellow
- berate
- blab
- broadcast
- chattering
- chatty
- comment
- conversation
- converse
- conversing
- cry
- cuss
- declaration
- declare
- decry
- diction
- disclosing
- discuss
- discussing
- enunciating
- explain
- express
- expressing
- expression
- gab
- gossip
- insult
- mention
- narrate
- orating
- outspoken
- proclaim
- pronouncing
- pronunciation
- ranting
- repeating
- report
- reproach
- say
- saying
- scold

- shout
- speak
- speaking
- speech
- spouting
- state
- swear
- talking
- tell
- translating
- utterance
- verbalization
- vocalization
- voicing
- whisper
- yell

Listening
- accent
- attune
- audible
- deaf
- deafen
- earful
- eavesdropping
- hear
- hearsay
- hush
- hushed
- inaudibility
- listen
- musical
- muted
- noise
- overhear
- overtones
- phonetics

- quiet
- record
- rumour
- silence
- speechless
- unhearing

Sound quality
- acoustic
- acoustics
- alto
- baritone
- bass
- cadence
- intensity
- intonation
- loudness
- pitch
- raspy
- resound
- reverberate
- reverberation
- soprano
- sound
- tempo
- tenor
- timbre
- tone
- vibration
- voice
- volume

Sound effects
- bang
- bash
- blast
- boom

- buzz
- clang
- clapping
- clatter
- click
- crack
- drumming
- echo
- explosion
- growl
- knock
- pop
- racket
- rattle
- ring
- roar
- rumble
- scraping
- screech
- shrillness
- siren
- slam
- slap
- snap
- squawking
- squeaking
- strumming
- thunder
- tinkling
- toot
- twang
- uproar
- wham
- whistle

Things that make sound
- accordion

- alphorn
- bagpipes
- banjo
- bell
- castanets
- cello
- chimes
- clarinet
- cymbals
- didgeridoo
- drum
- flute
- gong
- guitar
- harp
- horn
- marimba
- oboe
- piano
- rattle
- saxophone
- tambourine
- triangle
- trombone
- trumpet
- tuba
- ukulele
- violin
- xylophone
- zither
- any musical instrument or thing that makes sound

Phrases
- all ears
- be heard
- blabbermouth
- call on
- chatty Cathy
- clear as a bell
- clearly expressed
- describe in detail
- double-talk
- express yourself
- give an account of
- give me your ear
- grant an audience
- heard voices
- hidden message
- hold your tongue
- idle talk
- in earshot
- in full cry
- just clicked
- keynote speaker
- loud and clear
- make music
- manner of speaking
- plain-spoken
- power of speech
- purrs like a kitten
- rap session
- rat-a-tat
- rings a bell
- state your purpose
- strain of melody
- tattletale
- tell me
- to tell the truth
- tongue-tied
- tune in/tune out
- unheard of
- voice an opinion

In Business

When you want people with auditory in the communication zone to hear your proposal or point of view, the tone of voice to ensure understanding is fast, excited, and with a certain amount of intensity to it. Remember, how you say things—the tone, timbre, volume, speed, and intensity—is important to the person with auditory in the communication zone. For example:

- "When I tell you the facts, if this *resonates* with you, we could go ahead and *discuss* how to set it up."
- "If this proposal *sounds good* to you, we can *talk* about implementing it."

Personal Interactions

In personal interactions with people with auditory in the communication zone, it's helpful to use a firmer voice to be taken seriously. Using auditory words helps them to understand you better:

- "Can you tell me what works for you?"
- "Does getting together next Sunday sound good to you?"

You also need to really pay attention and listen to their response, because this to an auitory communicator is a sign of respect.

Important Question

The most important questions for people with auditory in the communication zone are *where* and *what if* questions. Such questions help them to determine the value of the information, product, skill, or service, which in turn determines their direction. For example:

- Where is it applicable?
- Where is it useful?
- What if we used this to …?
- What if we applied it to …?

If something is determined to be not useful, not practical, or less than the quality their standards demand, they will throw it out, dismiss it, or give it little to no value.

Learning

People with auditory in the communication zone learn by discussing things and understanding where learning is applicable. They must understand something before they can accept it. They are practical-minded and need to know where they can apply new information or skills they are learning. If they can't apply it, they don't value it.

These individuals can repeat things back to you easily and learn well by listening. Programs on audiobooks, online classes, or the internet are good for them. They can enjoy talking on the phone, so coaching by phone or Skype are other ways of learning that may appeal to them.

People with auditory in the communication zone like to be told how they are doing and respond to certain tones of voice. Remember that with these learners, *how* something is said—the intensity, tone, tempo, timbre, and volume—is of paramount importance. They will be interested in the usefulness of the ideas, improvements, or the way in which they can apply the material that they are learning. If this is not readily apparent, they will lose interest.

In the classroom, students with auditory in the communication zone can't sit still for long and would benefit from regular breaks with physical exercise. As children, they are often misdiagnosed with ADHD or other learning disabilities. If the teacher doesn't have a certain level of vocal intensity or is too soft-spoken, or if those with auditory in the communication zone don't understand how the information will be useful, they will not pay attention. If they have been sitting still for too long, they will start to fidget or become a distraction in the class.

Because they are so good with ideas, these individuals will generate some in order to amuse themselves or the class, and they can be quite a handful for the teacher who doesn't know how to channel their creative energy or motivate them to stay on task. Routine bores them, and they need a lot of variety and challenge to be inspired. They often push the edges of authority, not recognizing authority outside themselves. It is typical for them to feel that the rules are unfair or uncalled for and to have no respect for authority figures who impose them.

Major Personality Challenges

Of all the communication zones, people with auditory in the communication zone are the most misunderstood. Because they are overtly intense and often loud, they can appear too serious, intense, aggressive, negative, or angry, even when they are not actually feeling that way at all.

Their biggest challenge is diplomacy, and others often have difficulty receiving their factual, direct, or even blunt way of saying things without being offended. When it is pointed out to auditory communicators that they have given offence, it confuses them, as they think they were being clear and to the point. Often, they think other people are just too sensitive. They truly embrace the "fix it or forget it" attitude and don't like to get caught up in the drama.

People with auditory in the communication zone can be exceedingly quick to frustration in any given situation and impatient with those who do not readily understand things from just the facts. They can go from friendly to ferocious in the blink of an eye.

If they are not being physically active in their life, or if they aren't being engaged in accomplishing something, or if they are bored with what they are doing, the chatter in the mind of the person with auditory in the communication zone can quickly spiral into negative thought patterns. These thinking patterns can go around and around obsessively like a gerbil on a wheel, and it's hard for the individual to stop without some sort of energy release, usually in the form of explosive or aggressive behaviour.

It is harder on the person with auditory in the communication zone to do nothing than to be extremely busy. Being physically active or releasing artistically with sound (as in drumming or another musical outlet) or doing something that combines the two (such as chopping wood, which is both physical and has the satisfying sound of cracking wood, or playing squash, which is physical, aggressive, and they get to hit something), helps the person with auditory in the communication zone stay in balance or get back into balance.

Career/Organizations

People with auditory in the communication zone tend to demand the lead position. They love challenges and like to conquer each one for the joy of it. They can be very competitive. They are real go-getters and are often pioneers and innovators in their chosen field. They are spearheads; they like to go in and shake things up, start new projects, or get the show on the road. They have a strong sense of inner authority, find it easy to direct others, and are good at delegation. They love to put their ideas into action, but prefer to delegate most of the detail work so they can move on to new challenges. They see themselves as catalysts to get things moving. They are intense leaders and may not be the most diplomatic ones.

At the same time, they can have a deep and genuine love for their fellow humans and the world, which radiates out through warmth and caring. They can get along well with people and be good leaders because they value self-respect, respect for others, and free will. They trust that others can and will do their part.

Those with auditory in the communication zone expect that others will need only the facts and the end goal, and with these will work independently without much supervision. They feel it would be insulting to others to give them all the details or tell them how they think it should be done, and they can be surprised and irritated when they find that others need more information or supervision. They may even be a bit arrogant or condescending if they feel the other person is asking what to them appear to be obvious questions. They often do not understand that some people need the details to get a feeling for the project.

They easily dish out pressure to others but do not work well under pressure themselves. They have a tendency to feel insulted if you ask why or question how they are doing something and can be quite abrupt and blunt in their reply. They need to have a sense of accomplishing things in order to get fulfilment from what they are doing. They place value on themselves and their work according to the financial reward they receive, and they demand respect for their work. They won't often waste time on anything that is not going to help them in some way.

Because their energy is so strong and intense, they need to be alert that they do not stray into power-tripping, for this can cause all kinds of communication problems. Other processing styles may be so intimidated by the person with auditory in the communication zone that they won't ask the questions they need to ask to get the job done. Or, when asked for their opinion, other processing styles will give the answer they think the person with auditory in the communication zone wants rather than their real opinion. In working relationships, auditory communicators need to learn to ask what is needed and make requests rather than demanding or commanding that things be done.

Amusement and Humour

The person with auditory in the communication zone loves to poke fun and stir the pot. Jokes and humour are second nature to these individuals—and often of the sarcastic variety. They can be the biggest teasers and are not always aware of how others are reacting. This can sometimes lead to hurt feelings.

Because of their intense nature, they sometimes don't realize that they have gone too far. They are the ones who watch those shows where people have accidents, do stunts, or embarrass themselves and then get great laughs from all the shenanigans. They enjoy slapstick or physical humour, like the Three Stooges. Shows that play with ideas and politics, like *Saturday Night Live*, are very funny to them. Again, they like variety and are bored quickly.

Decisions

If they understand things and have the facts, the person with auditory in the communication zone is usually discerning and quick to make a decision. Being information-oriented, these individuals need to have and understand all of the facts before making a decision. If the relevant facts are not all there or if they do not have the understanding, they will not make a decision.

Physical Space

Quality, simplicity, and practicality characterize the lifestyle of people with auditory in the communication zone. They like things to be useful, while at the same time, they like things that are of high quality. Generally, things are put in their practical places where they can be used with a minimum of fuss and bother and will accommodate an economy of motion. Things in their environment are evaluated on the basis of practicality, usefulness, amusement, simplicity, quality, and whether or not it's on the leading edge of technology. If something is no longer useful, usually they recycle, repurpose, or get rid of it.

Physiology

Breathing

The breathing of people with auditory in the communication zone is fairly rhythmic and steady, and you will notice they breathe from the middle of their chest.

Movement

Generally, their movement when talking or lecturing is minimal—and when there is movement, it is used with precision and economy, unless they are nervous; then they will fidget or pace. Most of the time, they are quite efficient in their movement. This is like the lion conserving its energy even though the rabbit is nearby; the lion will not get up to chase the rabbit because that would use up more energy than it would gain from eating the rabbit.

Those with auditory in the communication zone are highly physical when it is required and prefer to be active. If they have to sit still for longer periods of time, they will be genuinely uncomfortable and would need to get up and move or get fidgety. They would rather talk to you while walking or gardening or doing something they deem to be important so they are accomplishing something while chatting.

Gestures

Their gestures are mid-body, usually between the waist and shoulders. Often the gestures are rhythmic. Most gestures are used to emphasize a point.

Physicality

People with auditory in the communication zone will often tilt their head (telephone position) when listening. They will punctuate their speech with *ahs* or *ums* and are easily distracted by noise. They are very active; they are doers. They have a unique way of moving their eyes sideways back and forth as they listen to their inner dialogue.

Even in relaxation or rest, these individuals exude an energy of intensity. Auditory communicators do not have to look at you to talk to you or to hear you when you are talking. They will often continue with a task; they may even talk to you from another room or from an area separate from you.

Out-of-Balance Tendencies

There seems to be no middle ground: when people with auditory in the communication zone go out of balance, they think in extremes. They either act like a raging bull in a china shop or become totally withdrawn, giving you the silent treatment. They are likely to blurt out things without diplomacy, often saying things they don't mean or saying aggressive things which they later don't remember saying. At these times, they may also seem to lose their ears, because they appear not to hear a word you are saying.

This is when they can appear aggressive and even hostile. It's an understatement to say that those with auditory in their communication zone are good at anger—they are experts on rage. With their short fuse, they can be aggressive, rude, blunt, and as difficult to get along with as a bear with a sore paw.

They are expert at exerting mental pressure with the silent treatment, which can go on for hours, days, and even weeks. They become quite insecure and can put out a veneer of indifference to keep anyone from becoming too intimate. In this out-of-balance state, they usually don't want to be touched physically because they interpret physical touch as a form of control or manipulation. They can be as stubborn as a mule.

In their imbalanced state, they must have their own way, and they are able at times to apply pressure to others with an intensity that seems to be without mercy. They are not above threatening or implanting fear to get their own way. Demanding and determined that their way will rule, they will even use humiliation to control others.

When these individuals are out of balance, not only are they often unaware of what they are saying, they have difficulty remembering their words, and only remember what their intent in the argument or disagreement was. As a result, they can add insult to injury by denying that they said what they did, which makes others feel like they are lying. At such times, their tolerance for others' differences becomes sadly lacking, and they can demand everyone understand the situation their way.

Although they can dish out pressure, they absolutely cannot take pressure themselves. If people with auditory in the communication zone are feeling pressure, then anyone around them will also be feeling it. They have real difficulty admitting they are wrong and may never admit it. If you cross them, watch out—these individuals hold resentments for a long time and are quick to seek vengeance. They may forgive, but they never forget.

People with auditory in the communication zone can at times be possessive of their partner/spouse and their things. They can find it difficult to be alone, because their minds go into a negative spiral. Often, this becomes about finances, but it can be about almost any negative idea which they twist and twist and can't seem to let go of without significant effort. Having their finances in order and having a little nest egg for emergencies also helps them to stay in balance.

When it comes to blame and blaming, out-of-balance auditory communicators are wizards at it. Nothing is their fault or their problem; there is always someone or something else to blame. At the same time, those with auditory in the communication zone seldom complain, and when out of balance, they have absolutely no tolerance for complainers. Even when in balance, they find grumblers hard to be around.

When out of balance, auditory communicators find it hard to complete projects. They get caught up in the details and lose sight of the big picture. They also lack orderliness in their approach. In their frustration at not accomplishing what they wanted, they can be quite abrasive.

These individuals need to be exceptionally physically active, with at least three really good, break-a-sweat workouts a week—more if they can. This helps to control the physical build-up of auditory energy and intensity. Doing concentrated physical activity takes the edge off, so to speak.

They need to have direction in their life and to have both long- and short-term goals. They need to be able to measure their accomplishments so they can get fulfilment from what they are doing. Finally, if they are missing information, people with auditory in the communication zone need to seek it out and make sure they understand what is going on. This helps to give them direction and security.

Review of Auditory in the Communication Zone

Highest Values

- fairness
- humanity
- practicality

Needs

- to be treated fairly
- to be active
- to have the facts
- to understand

- to have direction
- to be accomplishing
- to have their finances in order
- to be physically active
- to have an auditory outlet that allows them to make loud intense noise
- to have someone they can use as a sounding board
- to have alone time (can just be in another room in the house)

Challenges

- diplomacy
- external authority
- being questioned on why or how they are doing something
- not being paid what they think they are worth
- intensity
- aggression
- impatience
- quickness to frustration
- inaction
- negative compulsive thinking

How Others Describe Them

- humanitarians
- interesting
- determined
- bold
- competitive
- idea people
- inspiring
- productive
- high performers
- risk-takers
- outspoken
- intense
- aggressive
- undiplomatic
- bossy
- forceful
- blamers
- too serious
- too loud
- too angry
- aggressive
- repetitive
- insensitive
- scary
- confusing
- rude

Out-of-Balance Behaviours

- acting at the extremes with no middle ground
- either showing bull-like intensity or giving the silent treatment
- being emotionally withdrawn
- acting stubborn
- placing blame
- insisting on their way at all costs
- showing insensitivity to others
- dishing out pressure but being unable to take it
- controlling by fear
- holding on to resentment, possibly seeking vengeance
- blurting out words but not remembering later
- demanding
- being an expert at rage

Solutions to Create Balance

- Get active; challenge yourself.
- Engage in physical exercise. Sweat at least three times a week—more is better.
- Get the facts and pursue understanding.
- Create a direction.
- Create attainable goals you can achieve daily.
- Channel your energy into positive projects.
- Create or find a job where you are paid what you're worth.
- Get your financial records in good order.
- Get rid of useless junk or worn-out stuff.

Chapter 12
How to Quickly Identify the Different Communication Styles

Kinesthetic

People with kinesthetic in the communication zone:

- talk slower, pause more, and breathe more deeply
- usually gesture low, below the waist
- generally enjoy being around people
- are enthusiastic and stimulating
- are animated and active
- are very social
- encourage informality
- express emotional opinions
- talk in kinesthetic language
- need to be comfortable

If you're meeting with someone who has kinesthetic in the communication zone, it's important to slow your pace down. Breathe deeply and talk about the why of the situation, project, feelings, and actions. Actually change your voice tone and pace so that it matches theirs and really "get in touch with it." Kinesthetic words will help them get a feeling for what you are saying, and they will participate more. If you can give them a story which emphasizes what you are saying, even better.

Visual

People with visual in the communication zone:

- talk more quickly and excitedly, with shallow breaths
- usually gesture high, often above the shoulders
- give the appearance of being quiet and reserved
- listen attentively to other people
- tend to avoid the use of power
- make decisions in a thoughtful and deliberate manner
- are often light-hearted, warm, and compliant

If you're meeting with someone who has visual in the communication zone and you are not a visual communicator, sit up in your chair, breathe from the top of your lungs, pick up the pace of your speech, and be slightly excited in your tone. At least act in a way that matches the pace of what the visual communicator is doing, and that individual will be more interested in what you have to say. If you then add in some visual words in the appropriate places, the communication will become clearer and this individual can better picture what you are saying. Painting a picture with your words assists the visual communicator. Having something to look at also helps.

Cognitive

People with cognitive in the communication zone:

- go through a range of paces in their speech patterns, fast to slow
- go through a full range of breathing, from top of the chest all the way down
- make a range of gestures, high to low
- say "I know" or "that makes sense" a lot
- control emotional expression
- prefer orderliness
- tend to express measured opinions
- seem difficult to get to know and appear reserved
- may appear preoccupied and stand-offish
- are precise, disciplined and industrious

If you meet a person who has cognitive in the communication zone, make sure you provide enough reasonable, logical information so this individual can make sense of what you are saying. Do this in an orderly, sequential fashion—*first this, then that,* or *A, B, C.* Match whatever verbal pace the cognitive communicator is using. Adding in cognitive words appropriately will also allow this individual to make sense of your communication. Make sure to answer the cognitive communicator's questions in a logical way, including your reasoning so the individual can make sense of it.

Auditory

People with auditory in the communication zone:

- talk at a moderate pace
- breathe from the mid-chest
- say "um" and "ah" a lot
- appear to be quite busy
- may give the impression of not listening

- display a serious attitude
- can appear aggressive and intense
- are bold, frank, and opinionated
- can be repetitive
- are very intense when excited or angry, sound loud, and are quick-speaking
- speak factually with a minimal amount of words

If you're meeting with someone who has auditory in the communication zone, it is important to be factual, intensify your energy slightly, modulate your voice, breathe from the middle of your chest, and listen—really listen. Meeting these individuals at their verbal pace and adding auditory words or sound effects where appropriate will allow them to tune in to your communication more and understand you better.

Part Four
The Challenge Zone

Read the description of this zone and then turn directly to your component or to the component of the person in this zone who you want to understand better. This is your backup system—the place you go internally when you are stressed and from where you can act externally from this out-of-balance stressed place.

Description

The component in our challenge zone determines how we react when we are challenged in life. Remember, the challenge zone is the part of our processing style that blends closely with our communication zone—the qualities of which add a richness to our communication and personality, often co-mingling in such a way that people might even think that this *is* our communication style. This blending adds another dimension to our personalities and presents our most important challenges to overcome.

We also use the challenge zone system as our backup check for the decisions we make. This is our secondary system, which helps us interpret the world around us. It is called the *challenge* zone because when we get stressed, we shift into the out-of-balance qualities of the component in this zone. As we become stressed, the out-of-balance tendencies become magnified, and we act from that place.

The more stressed we are, the more intensely we go into the out-of-balance qualities of that component. Those qualities can sometimes be magnified tenfold. When we are stressed, this is where we go internally. Our personality will be most challenged when we shift into the out-of-balance tendencies of our challenge zone—and the people around us will be challenged as well.

Other people with the same component in their communication zone that we have in our challenge zone can also challenge us greatly when we are in our stressed place. This is because we will see in them or they will reflect to us the things that are challenging us. When we are stressed, this affects us deeply, and we often have some difficulty returning to a balanced state. The good news is that there is always something we can do to bring ourselves back into balance.

Some say that to handle this part of our personality is to handle the shadow side of our nature. One positive way of looking at this is that this is the component we need to work on the most. Our challenge component is the part of our personality that we need to strive to master. As we master this, we master our biggest challenges.

Chapter 13
The Challenge Zone: Kinesthetic

When someone has the kinesthetic component in the challenge zone, that person possesses many of the qualities listed about kinesthetic in the communication zone (so reading the section on kinesthetic in the communication zone could be helpful). Remember, this zone blends with the communication zone. This is the secondary system—the backup system.

When the person is learning, having kinesthetic in this zone acts as a final check in the learning system, working with and blending with the primary learning system, which is the component in the communication zone. For people with kinesthetic in this zone as the secondary system, hands-on learning and walking through something a couple of times until they get a feeling for it gives them confidence in their learning and secures it in place.

Having kinesthetic in this zone becomes most challenging when the person is very stressed and, as a result, shifts into and lands hard in the out-of-balance qualities of the kinesthetic. These qualities become magnified.

When these individuals have shifted and landed hard in kinesthetic out-of-balance qualities, they begin to take everything personally. What is said, other people's reactions and behaviours—literally anything that is happening around them that they can feel something about, they may take personally or believe is directed at them. In this stressed state, they can become childish, defensive, or clingy. They may require continual reassurance.

Emotionally, these individuals can become acutely sensitive and discouraged. This can look to other people as if they are feeling sorry for themselves, complaining, whining, or wimping out. Often, they can go into an emotional wallow, allowing negative feelings to consume them.

When people with kinesthetic in the challenge zone are out of balance, they have difficulty accepting responsibility for themselves and can act helpless and uninformed in order to gain sympathy. If they are feeling bad, they want everyone around them to feel bad too; therefore, they can become quite manipulative or noticeably dramatic. When in this stressed state, they have a tendency to become childish, and if they are in pain (real or imagined), they will strike out verbally or physically to hurt another without any thought of the consequences. Most of the time, what is said or done is later regretted.

As comfort is one of the highest values for those with kinesthetic in the challenge zone, usually what they want is for discomfort to stop, at almost any cost. They will also stay in their suffering until they are ready to come out of it, so that attempts to make them feel better before they are ready to feel better will often fail.

If people with kinesthetic in the challenge zone are full of emotion, such that they can't take any more in, they will want to leave or get away from the situation. Because these individuals tend to take everything personally and are easily hurt, they are extremely sensitive and often pick up on other people's feelings and moods, even if it's not obvious. Because people who have kinesthetic in the challenge zone are so sensitive to others, one of their major challenges is boundaries and discernment of their feelings and other people's feelings: where do they begin and end, what are the boundaries, and whose feelings are they feeling? In particular, when stressed, having boundaries and setting boundaries can be a real challenge.

Sometimes talking out loud to someone who lends an empathetic ear, which allows them to work through their emotion, can get them out of the wallow. They do not necessarily have to understand what it is about; sometimes, just expressing the emotion can release it. Another way to assist the person out of the kinesthetic wallow and to come back into balance is to quit talking, because this just keeps adding to the pile of things they have to feel through and process. Also, you could give them a hug; physical affection without confusing words often speaks more loudly to them.

Reconnecting with those they care about and having fun are also ways to get back into balance for people with kinesthetic in the challenge zone. More importantly, being out of balance is a non-active state, so it is extremely important for them to get active—to move into action as soon as they can. Once they take action again, they begin to come back into balance and will return or shift back into their normal communication zone and the balanced qualities of the kinesthetic in the challenge zone.

When people with kinesthetic in the challenge zone are relaxed and in balance, this can contribute to them being sensitive, emotional, social, and tactile. They will be more affectionate, caring, and social people.

We make our decisions first in our communication zone, and once a decision has been made, we check with our backup system to confirm whether it's a good decision or not. With kinesthetic in the challenge zone as the backup system, the person wants to have a feeling about that decision before taking action on it. Sometimes this can happen extremely fast, and at other times, the person may need some time to gather more details to get a feeling about the decision. Once these individuals have a feeling in the challenge zone, they can take action on a decision or not, based on the feeling they get.

The kinesthetic component in the challenge zone can also create resistance to learning or doing new things, even if these individuals want to do new things. They may find resistance because they don't have a feeling for it yet. They will continue to look for the right information or a recommendation to give them the right feeling to move forward on what they are resisting.

The communication zone and the challenge zone and how they blend and work together are the predominant parts of our personality. This is the face we present to the world and how we are perceived by others in the world. A summary of balanced kinesthetic qualities for the person who has kinesthetic in the challenge zone—which blends with the communication zone—would look like this:

- emotionally based (at times)
- outgoing
- friendly
- conscientious
- empathetic
- emotionally sensitive
- tactile
- responsive to physical rewards
- often dedicated
- persevering when committed to a course of action
- comfortable in own clothing, environment, and situations

Harmony in their relationships is important to these individuals. Having fun and being social is a need, not just a want. The kinesthetic component in the challenge zone contributes a lot to being enthusiastic, animated, and energetic. Having the component in this zone can at times create a childlike nature that is playful with a sense of wonderment, and even periodically a certain naiveté. It can contribute to these individuals being more optimistic and trusting, with a tendency to look for the silver lining. However, at times, looking for the silver lining can cause them to stay in detrimental situations longer than they should.

When a person has kinesthetic in the challenge zone, it can be seen in the way communication is given and in body language. In the physiology of these individuals, you may notice the qualities of both the communication zone and the challenge zone. Kinesthetic in this zone can lead to slower speech patterns and also the use of kinesthetic words and phrases. See the section on kinesthetic in the communication zone for further detail.

Review of Kinesthetic Out-of-Balance Tendencies

Remember, for the person with kinesthetic in the challenge zone, these out-of-balance qualities can be magnified, sometimes tenfold.

Behaviours

- being in a non-active state
- taking everything personally
- being overly emotional or too sensitive
- being defensive and clingy
- requiring constant reassurance
- not taking responsibility for self
- wallowing around in the negative feeling and feeling sorry for self
- being dramatic
- complaining, whining, or wimping out
- being manipulative and at times very dramatic
- creating physical symptoms to avoid things
- acting childish
- disorganizing situations to create attention; needing attention
- staying in suffering until ready to come out
- wanting company in misery, so often spreading it around
- leaving or running away when full of emotion and unable to take more in, or stopping it at all costs

Solutions to Create Balance

- Take action. (Doing nothing makes it worse.)
- Have fun and be social.
- Reconnect with those you care about.
- Get physical affection without confusing words.
- Talk and process out loud to someone who is supportive and non-judgemental.

Chapter 14
The Challenge Zone: Visual

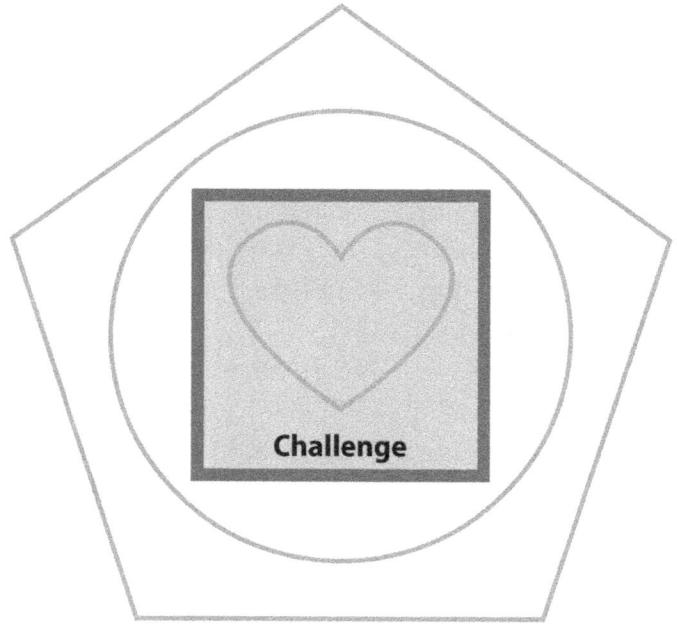

When someone has the visual component in the challenge zone, that person possesses many of the qualities described in the section on visual in the communication zone (reading that section could be helpful). This is the secondary system or backup system.

When the person is learning, visual in this position acts as the backup check, working and blending with the primary learning system, which is the component in the communication zone. So people with visual in the challenge zone as the secondary system need to get a clear picture of what it is they are learning. This gives them confidence in their learning and is the final step in their learning process. Demonstrations, a picture of what they are learning, or written material they can see is highly useful to them. Visually organized and even colour-coded materials are especially advantageous.

Having visual in the challenge zone becomes most difficult when these individuals are very stressed and go into the out-of-balance qualities of the visual. In this zone, the visual out-of-balance qualities become magnified. These individuals become extremely stubborn, inflexible, and rigid. They can get stuck in whatever picture/movie they have and seem totally inflexible or unable to see it differently.

If you are making changes to plans, projects, or their picture too quickly, they will become resistant and could even get a bit hostile or upset. Impatience with others or with information which has too much detail can also be hugely challenging. When stressed, people with visual in the challenge zone will create a huge issue with timing and become irritable because they want everyone to move on their schedule and get impatient when that doesn't happen. This can add stress to their relationships, and often they are unaware of it.

These individuals can become terribly bored if others are moving at a slower pace than theirs or taking too long on a particular subject. This can cause them to go off into their own movie, no longer paying attention or listening to what is going on.

When in the stressed out-of-balance qualities, they can become quite critical and judgemental. They will quickly spot errors in other people's work or ideas and think it's their duty to make corrections. Their need for perfection kicks in, taking over and making them their own worst enemy, for they are so critical of themselves that they can't take even the slightest criticism from someone else. Even a difference of opinion on something may be seen as a criticism or an attempt to make them wrong.

When they are out of balance, people with visual in the challenge zone can take a very tragic view of life because nothing seems to be meeting their expectations. Black-and-white thinking can become much more pronounced. When they slip into this stressed place, they become totally rule-driven and don't understand why everyone isn't playing by the same rules. The only "right way" of doing things is their way when they are in this out-of-balance state, as they cannot conceive of any other way until they come into a more balanced state.

When they are stressed, they may even recall a certain set of negative emotional memories or mental movies which they bring frequently to mind to punish themselves, creating a tired and confused state. Under extreme stress, they can withdraw into themselves and become depressed. They can become discouraged and disillusioned and may even give up. At this point, being reminded of the bigger picture and the things they can look forward to or do well can assist them out of that place.

If these individuals lack self-awareness, they can become quite anxious, worry a lot about little things, get stuck in the small picture, and become easily upset at almost anything. At times of stress, those with visual in the challenge zone have a tendency to not hear what others are saying or to have only very selective hearing when others are talking, which can result in misunderstandings. They may also over-exaggerate their emotional needs because they want to get their own way—which can result in them making unreasonable demands on others.

These individuals can't handle other people putting pressure—or what they perceive to be pressure—on them. They are so hyper-aware of how things look, they can go into over-the-top "clean and organize" mode. They may even have to leave if the environment they are in is too disorganized or out-of-harmony. When stressed, things like how they look, how their partners or children look, and how their home or car looks can be crazy-making for them if it doesn't fit their picture of how it should be.

To bring themselves back into balance, they need to get organized, set their priorities, and set a plan of action. They need to create a neat, clean, and orderly environment. They need to create something to look forward to, something to work towards—a goal. Sometimes a timeout or a mini-vacation is all that is needed.

Once a decision has been made using the component in the communication zone, the visual as the backup system in this zone will have the person checking on that decision based on how something appears. These individuals will need a clear picture of what that decision/goal will look like before they can take action on that decision. They will often do this so quickly that they don't necessarily even realize that this is a secondary step. Having the timing or a deadline for something assists them.

Remember that the communication zone and the challenge zone and how they blend and work together are the predominant parts of our personality. This is the face we present to the world and how we are perceived by others in the world.

A summary of balanced visual qualities for the person who has visual in the challenge zone—which blends with the component in the communication zone—would look like this: When in balance, having visual in the challenge zone:

- helps a person be organized
- makes a person good at planning
- gives an innate sense of balance and symmetry
- can increase an artistic approach to things
- enhances appreciation for beauty and nature.

Most of the time, these individuals realize the importance of not imposing on others, as they have a natural ability to see what it is like to walk in another person's shoes. This helps them establish rapport and good communication with people and assists them in being able to work with others easily.

Those with visual in the challenge zone are also going to be more concerned with how things look: how they personally look, how their environment looks, the look on the person's face who is talking to them, how their family or spouse looks, and how that reflects on them. With visual as the secondary system or backup system, how they interpret the world to a certain degree will be based on understanding, by seeing a clear picture of the subject or having a visual reference. With friends and people close to them, seeing outward manifestations of affection, notes/gifts, or spending time in each other's company is significant to them.

Fitting ideas and concepts into the bigger picture helps them to understand and be comfortable with those ideas and concepts. For example, I once had a client who was stressed. With visual in her challenge zone, she was really stuck in her smaller picture. Her picture was that she had only two options in her life: to stay with her boyfriend, with whom she was very unhappy, or go to back to her ex-husband, which she did not want to do. She couldn't see any other option. What I did was connect her back to the bigger picture by asking, "What about all of the other men on the planet? Could there be another man, somewhere in the world, who might be a partner you could consider?" It was really interesting when she popped out of her smaller picture and realized she had other options.

Having visual in the challenge zone contributes to a love of beauty and organization and to a need to be in environments that are aesthetically pleasing and well ordered. If the person is really disorganized, that is a sign of being stressed and out of balance. So ideally for this person, it would be great to realize that things are becoming disorganized and that this is a signal of being stressed. Then, if the individual could do some internal investigation as to what is stressful and deal with that stress, it would be easier to come back into balance.

People with visual in the challenge zone will translate everything into pictures or internal movies because, as their secondary system of understanding or learning, it assists them in solidifying things. Having visual in this zone will also contribute to people having more of a critical eye, which they use to see if something fits or not.

When the visual component is in the challenge zone, its blending can also be seen in the way communication is given and in body language. In the physiology, you may notice the qualities of both the communication zone and the challenge zone. An example would be the ability to process information very quickly, moving and talking more quickly, and also using visual words and phrases. See the section on visual in the communication zone for further details.

Review of Visual Out-of-Balance Tendencies

Remember, in the challenge zone, these out-of-balance qualities can be magnified, sometimes tenfold.

Behaviours

- being rigid
- lacking flexibility
- getting stuck in fixed pictures
- placing time pressure on self and others
- acting critical and judgemental
- getting stuck in black-and-white thinking
- feeling duty-bound to point out and correct others' mistakes
- insisting there's only one right way
- being unable to handle pressure
- over-exaggerating emotional needs
- worrying a lot
- focusing on old pictures of emotionally negative experiences
- getting stuck in the small picture

Solutions to Create Balance

- Get organized.
- Set priorities or make lists.
- Put together a plan of action.
- Clean up your environment.
- Have something to look forward to.
- Work towards goals.
- Take a timeout or a mini-vacation.
- Clarify things.
- Get back to the bigger picture.

Chapter 15
The Challenge Zone: Cognitive

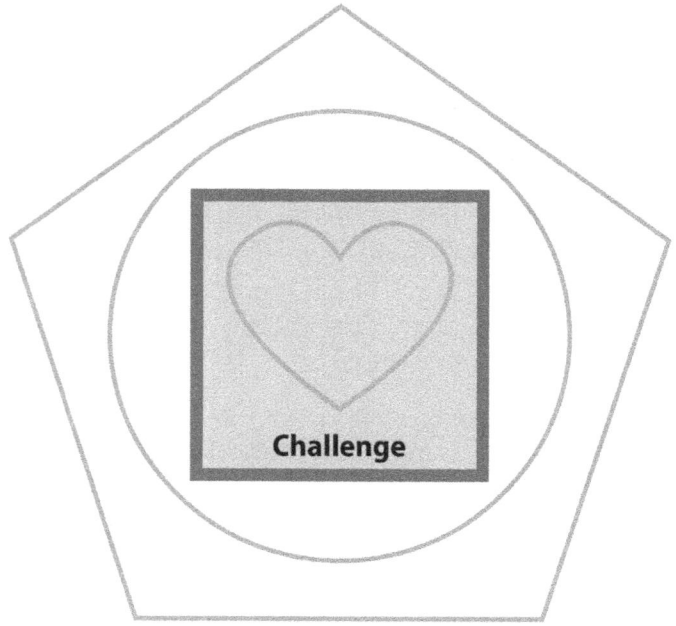

When someone has the cognitive component in the challenge zone, that person possesses many of the same qualities as cognitive is in the communication zone (reading the section on cognitive in the communication zone could be helpful). This is the secondary system or backup system.

When the person is learning, cognitive in this position acts as a backup check to the learning system, working and blending with the primary learning system—the component in the communication zone. People with cognitive in the challenge zone will want to make sense or give meaning and order to the lessons or information. In learning, they process by sequences and steps or procedures (such as *first step, second step*; *A, B, C*; or *1, 2, 3*). This gives them a sense of confidence and competence. Also, having cognitive in the challenge zone assists the individual in understanding where the learning or information fits in the bigger picture or the future.

Having cognitive in the challenge zone becomes most challenging when these individuals are very stressed, shift into the challenge zone, and go into the out-of-balance qualities of the cognitive. In this zone, the cognitive out-of-balance qualities become magnified.

When stressed, those with cognitive in the challenge zone may procrastinate or focus on how difficult it is to change their bad habits. They can become know-it-alls and have difficulty admitting when they are wrong about anything, for they seem to have a deep need to be right. They begin to isolate themselves and can spend too much time alone, sometimes not realizing that this is what is making them feel out of sorts.

Those with cognitive in the challenge zone, when stressed, have a major tendency towards escapism, which means they can do things to excess or extremes. For example, they could become addicted to alcohol, drugs, sex, porn, food, gambling, shopping, or even things like computers, reading, TV, or golf. Most of these activities are fine in moderation; it's only when those with cognitive in the challenge zone are stressed and in the out-of-balance qualities of the cognitive that this begins to happen. They need to be aware of this addictive tendency to avoid losing control of their lives.

These individuals can be very moody if they are not being creative in their lives. The more stressed they are, the more this is magnified. When out of balance, they can become aloof, arrogant, or argumentative. They can fear change and also be quite untrusting, even at times paranoid.

Those with cognitive in the challenge zone can become controlling if they are feeling out of control of their own life. They will want to control everything and everyone around them. Often, they can take on too many projects—more than they can effectively handle—and may overwhelm themselves.

In this out-of-balance, stressed place, they can at times appear to be overconfident or superior when they are actually upset. They can become the interrogator or a nosy parker with their questions. They can be extremely rebellious and rebel just for rebellion's sake. They are good at justification and can justify just about anything to themselves or when challenged.

When these individuals are out of balance, they can make mountains out of molehills because they often look for things to be more complex. They can make a big deal out of something trivial or mundane, overemphasizing the problem or difficulty until it becomes a real issue. When stressed, they can be quite intimidating. They seem to know exactly where to hit and how hard, picking up on the person's weakest area and using it to bring home their point.

When extremely stressed, those with cognitive in the challenge zone can have a tendency to be self-destructive. All of this changes as the person handles the stress and comes back into balance. Learning to focus on constructive thoughts and to reject the negative ones is important. Balancing social time along with appropriate alone time is a must. Asking constructive and productive questions is important, and learning to prioritize things and do them in an orderly fashion will be helpful in bringing this individual back into balance.

Remember that the communication zone and the challenge zone blend and work together as the predominant parts of our personality. This is the face we present to the world and how we are perceived by others in the world.

A summary of balanced cognitive qualities for the person who has cognitive in the challenge zone—which blends with the communication zone—would look like this:

- With cognitive the secondary system or backup system, to a certain degree how these individuals interpret the world will be based on gathering information, analysing, and trying to make sense out of the world around them. This helps them feel secure with the decisions they are making.
- Often, they just know things. They don't always know how they know. It's like having a sixth sense.
- Words can be extremely important. Those with cognitive in the challenge zone will pay more attention to the words you use and expect you to mean what you say.
- A strong sense of sensuality comes with having the cognitive component in the challenge zone. Enjoying good food, good sleep, and good sex assists these individuals in being less stressed.
- It is important that they eat breakfast, lunch, and dinner religiously and have protein with each meal. They should never have an important discussion with anyone unless they have eaten.

- Integrity—being in integrity with self and having others be in integrity with them—is hugely important.
- Honesty, trustworthiness, and being genuine are also important.
- They will take an interest in what people close to them are doing and ask questions because they like to know what is going on and to "be in the know."
- Having a future plan and knowing the direction they are going helps them to be less stressed.
- Having cognitive in the challenge zone contributes to their ability to be diplomatic and their ability to use words well.
- It contributes to their creativity and their ability to finish the tasks they start. Having closure is also important to them.
- They may prefer to be in environments where they have a certain sense of autonomy or independence and can do things in their own unique way.
- They may make sense out of everything because, as the secondary system of understanding or learning, the cognitive component assists them in knowing internally what is right for them.
- Having cognitive in the challenge zone can also cause people to be quite direct or to the point. They may at times shoot from the hip, so to speak.

When the cognitive component is in the challenge zone, its blending can also be seen in the way communication is given and in body language. In the physiology, you may notice qualities of both the communication zone and the challenge zone. Examples would be the care given to the words being used and use of more complicated sentences. There is a range of movement in their gestures, tempo of speech, and breathing. They use distinct sequencing and ordering, such as *first this, then that* or dates and data. They may use cognitive words and phrases. See the section on cognitive in the communication zone for further details.

Review of Cognitive Out-of-Balance Tendencies

Remember, in the challenge zone, these out-of-balance qualities can be magnified, sometimes tenfold.

Behaviours

- self-isolating
- procrastinating
- controlling
- being a know-it-all
- engaging in escapist behaviour
- rebelling
- Intimidating
- needing to be right
- feeling overwhelmed
- acting self-righteous
- being moody

Solutions to Create Balance

- Prioritize.
- Make a future plan.
- Create order.
- Create routine.
- Gather missing information.
- Create appropriate downtime.
- Balance alone time or create some alone time.
- Be creative or create an outlet to be creative.
- Know it's okay to not know something. (Get comfortable with this.)
- Ask yourself empowering questions.
- Focus on positive constructive thoughts and reject negative ones.
- Complete unfinished projects.
- Find closure if needed.
- Take time to dream or meditate.
- Explore your sensuality.

Chapter 16
The Challenge Zone: Auditory

When someone has the auditory component in the challenge zone, that person possesses many of the qualities which are described when auditory is in the communication zone (reading the section on auditory in the communication zone could be helpful). This is the secondary system or backup system.

When the person is learning, auditory in this position acts as a backup check to the learning system, working and blending with the primary learning system, which is the component in the communication zone. With auditory as the secondary system, people will want to understand how things work, or how things are, and most importantly where they can apply the learning or information to a situation or life.

Having auditory in the challenge zone becomes most challenging when these individuals are very stressed and shift into the challenge zone, going into the out-of-balance qualities of the auditory. In this zone, the auditory out-of-balance qualities become magnified, and these individuals seem to go to extremes. They can be aggressive, unapproachable, or quickly angered or frustrated. For example, they may give someone the silent treatment or be like an erupting volcano about something.

When stressed and out of balance, those with auditory in this zone find their biggest challenge is diplomacy and the tendency to blurt things out without forethought. As politeness goes out the window, the volume of their voice can rise and their tone may become harsh, sarcastic, or condescending. They do not hear themselves and often will not remember what they've said in the heat of the moment. They may even say after the fact, "I didn't say that," because they really don't remember saying it.

In most cases, these individuals are unaware that their volume and tone have changed—or if they are aware, they have no idea how intense they are being. To compound this, they become hypersensitive to others' tone and volume of voice and how others are responding to them.

A common thing that happens is that they will be told by the person they are communicating with to "stop yelling at me," and they will say something like "This isn't yelling" (loudly) and then "I can show you what yelling is" (getting even louder). Therefore, it is important for those who have auditory in the challenge zone to understand that if someone says you are yelling or raising your voice or talking in a harsh tone, even though you think you are not, you probably are.

When out of balance, if people with auditory in the challenge zone are not outwardly aggressive, they may be imploding on themselves. This will often happen with negative repetitive thought patterns which compulsively go around and around in their head. When stressed and out of balance, these individuals are also big into blaming and not taking responsibility for their actions or situation.

Finances are another area of concern for those with auditory in the challenge zone. When they are stressed, finances can become the targeted hot topic, even if that is not what is really stressing them. The other thing that can happen is that these individuals can go unconscious about finances, moving into avoidance and ignoring what is going on with their finances or bills. They can even spend money they don't have or avoid opening their bills, which only makes the situation worse.

When they are stressed, unwanted sounds will drive these individuals to distraction and cause them great irritation. For instance, if they live near a very busy street, the noise may be manageable when they are not stressed, but when they are stressed, this noise seems to be louder and more intense, causing them great irritation.

Those with auditory in the challenge zone, when stressed and out of balance, can really dish out pressure. They control others by using their anger or intensity and the fear this creates. If someone is pressuring them, though, they cannot handle it and will leave, go silent, or explode.

When people with auditory in the challenge zone are very stressed, they will have a physical build-up of excess energy. This energy is looking for a place to go, and it will either explode or implode until they learn to manage that energy and discharge it in a healthy way.

One of the ways to manage this energy is to be physically active and to actively sweat at least three times a week. Another is to be on top of finances, and another is to do something that has an auditory or sound component to it, such as playing a musical instrument or chopping wood. Engaging in a physical activity that has some aggression and noise, such as playing squash or tennis, is another good way to discharge that unwanted excess energy.

Remember that the communication zone and the challenge zone and how they blend and work together make up the predominant parts of our personality. This is the face we present to the world and how we are perceived by others in the world.

A summary of balanced auditory qualities for the person who has auditory in the challenge zone—which blends with the component in the communication zone—would look like this:

- How they interpret the world will, to a certain degree, be based on having all the facts they need to understand what is going on so they can feel secure in the decision they are making.
- Paying close attention to how something is said—the tone, tempo, and volume of voice—is important to them.

- They generally like having background music or white noise on, as this helps them stay relaxed and less stressed.
- They can often listen to someone talking to them while still continuing to do other work.
- Often, they have lots of ideas and can bounce from one to another.
- They enjoy brainstorming ways to do something better or more practically than before.
- Accomplishment is important.
- The ability to spearhead or get a project going, or to take practical action, is one of the strengths of those with auditory in the challenge zone.

When the auditory component is in the challenge zone, its blending can also be seen in the way communication is given and in body language. In the physiology, you may notice both the qualities of the communication zone and the challenge zone. An example would be the intensity of the message these individuals are delivering. Whether in anger, passion, or even relaxation, the auditory component is intense, even though they themselves are often oblivious to it. The auditory component is also good for making sound effects or using sound effects, and these individuals can use *um* or *ah* almost as punctuation. Gestures and breathing are usually mid-body or chest. They may also use auditory language and phrases.

Review of Auditory Out-of-Balance Tendencies

Remember, in the challenge zone, these out-of-balance qualities can be magnified, sometimes tenfold.

Behaviours

- acting at the extremes with no middle ground
- barging in like a bull in a china shop
- erupting like a volcano or giving the silent treatment
- being emotionally withdrawn
- acting stubborn
- placing blame
- insisting on one's own way at all costs
- showing insensitivity to others
- dishing out pressure
- controlling by fear
- holding on to resentment, possibly seeking vengeance
- blurting out words but not remembering later
- demanding
- being expert at rage

Solutions to Create Balance

- Get active and challenge yourself.
- Engage in physical exercise with an auditory component. Sweat at least three times a week—more is better.
- Get the facts.
- Pursue understanding.
- Accomplish things.
- Create attainable goals you can achieve daily.
- Channel your energy into positive projects.
- Create or find a job where you are paid what you're worth.
- Get your financial records in good order.
- Have a financial nest egg for emergencies.
- Get rid of useless junk or worn out stuff.

Part Five
The Security Zone

Read the description of this zone and then turn directly to your component or the component of the person who you want to understand better. This is where we go internally to create security and feel secure, and when we are feeling insecure, we go into the out-of-balance traits of the component in this zone.

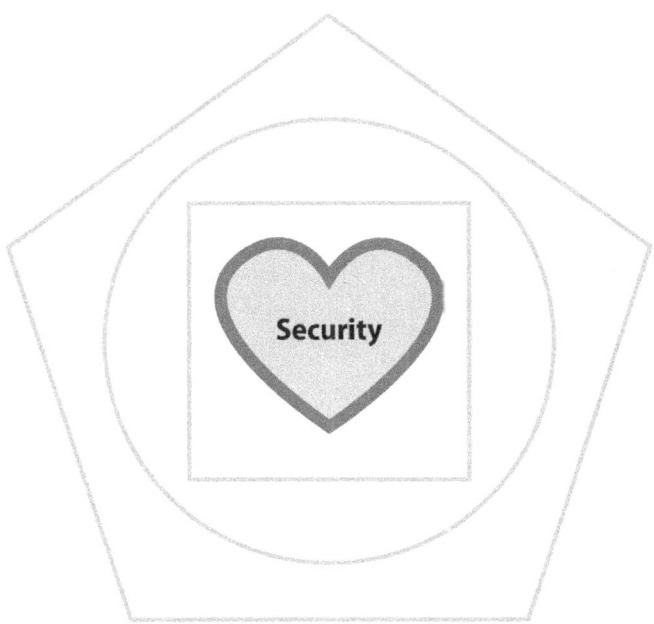

Description

The following is a detailed description of each of the four components and how they process and operate in the security zone. For each of the components in this zone, you'll find a description of the related tendencies, behaviours, and qualities. Remember, the security zone is the zone we go to in order to create security in our lives. It's our safe place. It is how we create security, both internally and externally.

It also determines how we react and respond when we feel insecure. When we are insecure and shift into this place inside ourselves, we often communicate and act from the out-of-balance tendencies of this component, both internally and externally. When we feel secure and are doing things that create security for ourselves, the out-of-balance qualities of this component are not present.

This is significantly different from what happens when the component is in the communication, challenge, or environmental zone. When the component is in the security zone, it is subtle and almost hidden until we go into the insecure, out-of-balance tendencies, which are not normally present. Then our behaviour stands out because it is not normally associated with us on a day-to-day basis, even though we ourselves are very familiar with it. It is normal for people to go in and out of feeling secure depending on what is happening in their lives.

Chapter 17
The Security Zone: Kinesthetic

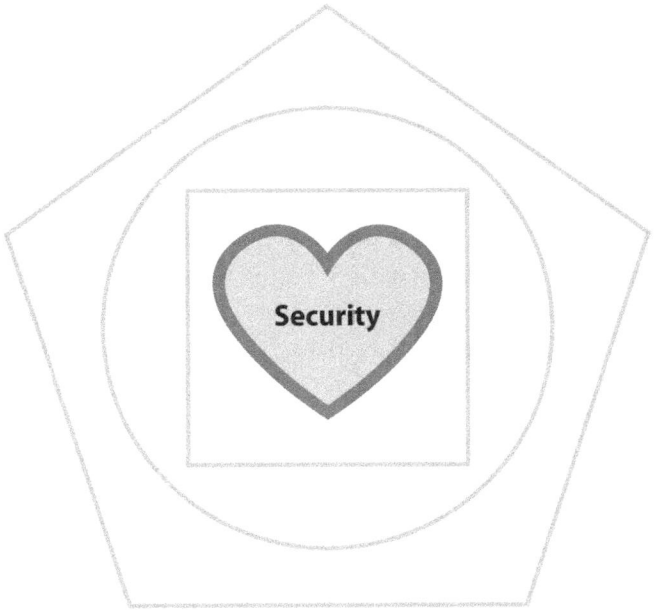

When a person has the kinesthetic component in the security zone, many of the qualities described in the section on kinesthetic in the communication zone can be present, but not in an obvious way. The emotional sensitivity here is subtler and not as overt as when a person has it in the communication or challenge zone. Decisions are not based on emotion, although if these individuals are secure in the decision they've made, they may feel good about it.

People with the kinesthetic component in the security zone are not generally overly emotional unless they are feeling insecure. It is important to these individuals that they feel connected with those they care about and feel close to, because having comfortable and harmonious relationships gives them a secure base in life. Having fun and being social can also bring them a great deal of security.

Taking action on things is extremely important when these individuals want to create more security for themselves. If they can take action on the things they are avoiding doing or take action on the things that are causing them to feel insecure, even better. Generally, just beginning to take action on *anything* will make them start to feel better, and not taking any action will prolong the feelings of insecurity.

Being comfortable in situations or with people is especially important to make them feel secure. Reassurance and physical affection can add to their security base. On the flip side, they can often feel insecure if they are arguing or out of sorts with those they care about. Feeling out of place, disconnected, or uncomfortable in situations or with certain people can cause insecurity.

When those with kinesthetic in the security zone are not feeling totally secure about something, talking through things out loud or taking the time to process and come to a feeling could be helpful. When these individuals become insecure for any reason, they begin to take everything personally, something that is not very present when they feel secure. They go into the out-of-balance qualities of the kinesthetic and can become childish, overly emotional, defensive, clingy, complaining, dramatic, manipulative, self-pitying, or overcome by negative emotions.

Usually in this out-of-balance state, people with kinesthetic in the security zone stop taking action or responsibility. This is significantly different from the individual's normal behaviour, and so it is noticeable when it occurs. Reconnecting with loved ones, taking action, getting comfortable, and having fun are at the top of the list for this individual to get back into balance and feel secure.

Ways to Create Balance and Security

- Move into action, action, action.
- Have fun, fun, fun.
- Take some space and time alone to feel things through.
- Reconnect with those you care about.
- Enjoy physical affection without confusing words.
- Create comfort in your clothes, environment, and relationships.

Chapter 18
The Security Zone: Visual

When the visual component is in the security zone, many of the qualities which are described in the visual component of the communication zone can be present. In fact, some may be more pronounced or emphasized, particularly around the areas of home, family, personal appearance, and how others may view us.

This is different from the visual component in the communication zone, where everything visual is important. For the person with visual in the security zone, it is more about them and how they look, how the things that pertain to them appear, or how the things that reflect upon them look. These can cause them to feel secure or insecure.

When people with visual in the security zone are around others, the way other people, places, or homes appear doesn't really matter—except, of course, if they feel it reflects on them. These individuals need to look the part, whatever they deem it to be, and be appropriately costume-ized. If they are going to a BBQ, they want to look like they are going to a BBQ; if they are going to the opera, they want to look like they are going to the opera, and wearing what they deem to be the appropriate clothing will help them feel secure. (Note: this is their interpretation, their picture, of what is appropriate)

Sometimes, if they are feeling really secure, their personal appearance may not matter to them; yet if they are at all insecure, or if they are wanting to avoid feeling insecure, it will. Being organized, tidy, and having a plan are all ways those with visual in the security zone stay secure. For instance, if they have people coming over to their home, they may go into a cleaning frenzy and get very perfectionistic about how things look.

Balance and harmony in their environment and their relationships help create security for those with visual in the security zone. Having things to look forward to, having things fit their picture, and moving in their own timing create security. Following family traditions or creating their own family traditions are additional steps in establishing their security foundation. Being recognized in a positive evaluation or for something they have done, even a thank-you, increases their level of security.

When those with visual in the security zone feel insecure, they shift into the out-of-balance qualities of the visual, becoming rigid and inflexible. *Stubborn* is the word that comes to mind, and what is really going on for them is they are stuck or fixated on their internal picture. They can often get stuck in the small picture and be unable in that moment to see the bigger one.

They can become black-and-white in their thinking and quite critical and judgemental in their outlook. They can become perfectionistic and create a lot of worry and anxiety. As mentioned earlier, cleaning their home or office or other spaces will create security. Doing something for themselves which causes them to look better in their own eyes—like buying new shoes or a new outfit for an occasion—creates more security. Getting organized, having something to look forward to, or making a plan will pull them into a more secure place inside.

Ways to Create Balance and Security

- Be appropriately dressed and costume-ized.
- Be organized.
- Clean and organize your work, home, or environment.
- Create an action plan.
- Make a list and set deadlines.
- Focus on your top three priorities; once you have accomplished these, move on to the next three.
- Get in touch with the bigger picture.

Chapter 19
The Security Zone: Cognitive

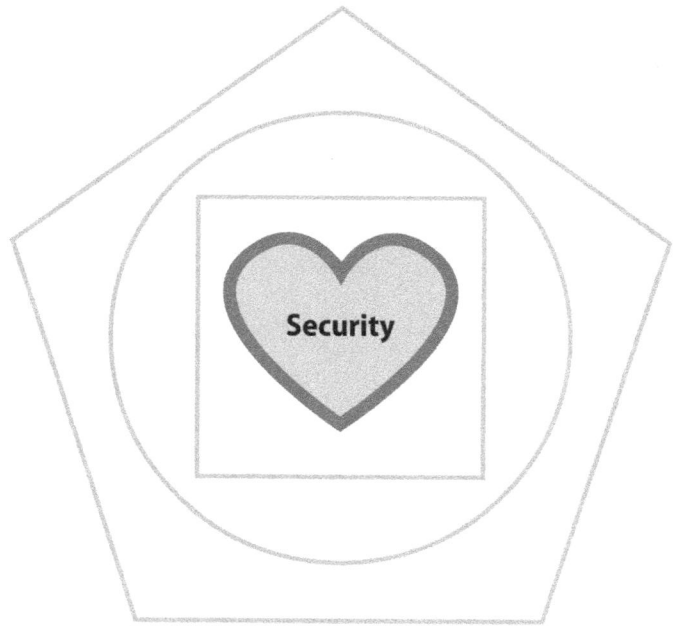

When the cognitive component is in the security zone, many of the qualities which are described in the section on cognitive in the communication zone can be present, and sometimes in quirky ways. For instance, people with cognitive in the security zone feel more secure if they have their favourite foods or comfort foods in the house—and can feel quite insecure when they aren't there. If you are the one doing the shopping, you may not notice this about yourself, because you would always ensure you had your comfort foods available.

Gathering information and making sense out of what is going on assists these individuals in creating a strong sense of security. Having closure on things is also important. Creating a future plan can assist them in becoming more secure. Having a sense of independence, choice, and integrity with themselves and others is an important part of creating a solid foundation of security. Someone with cognitive in the security zone needs a certain amount of alone time and some kind of creative outlet.

Good food, good sleep, and good sex can play a pivotal role in creating security for those with cognitive in the security zone. Sometimes if the sex is good, even if everything else is falling apart in the relationship, the person may stay because of a false sense of security.

Those with cognitive in the security zone will often feel much more secure if they know what is going on around them or know what is happening with the people they care about, even if it doesn't have anything to do with them. Trust is extremely important, and if that is broken, they can become like detectives tracking down the truth.

When people with cognitive in the security zone get insecure and shift into the out-of-balance qualities of the cognitive, they can go into isolating, procrastinating, controlling, rebellious, and righteous behaviours. They can become know-it-alls or can be intimidating. They may also go into escaping behaviours and overindulge in food, alcohol, drugs, porn, or sex. Other forms of escapism may come into play, such as working, reading, shopping, or using the computer or technology too much.

All of the following will help these individuals come back into balance and be more secure:

- gathering missing information and making sense of things
- having a future plan and starting on the first step
- creating order out of chaos
- being creative
- completing incomplete projects
- having closure
- asking empowering questions
- taking time to dream or meditate
- shopping for comfort foods

Ways to Create Balance and Security

- Get the necessary information to make sense of a situation.
- Have your comfort foods in the house.
- Connect sexually with your partner.
- Get a good night's sleep.
- Quit avoiding and start acting on what you know you need to do.
- Take some alone time.
- Be creative.
- Ask yourself empowering questions.

Chapter 20
The Security Zone: Auditory

When the auditory component is in the security zone, many of the qualities which are described in the section on the auditory component of the communication zone can be present. Having a certain level of intensity and a certain practicality go hand in hand when auditory is in the security zone. Understanding things, having all the facts, being treated fairly, and having an outlet for ideas and physical energy are all important in creating a solid foundation in security for those with auditory in this zone.

It is critical for these individuals to get the facts about their finances or get their finances in good order. Having a financial cushion, even a small one in case of emergency, will do wonders for their level of internal security.

Being active and accomplishing things is a good way to create security. Getting physically active and sweating at least three times a week can help to manage that intense auditory energy, and if it has a sound component to it, all the better (an example would be playing squash or tennis). Having someone they can use as a sounding board to bounce their ideas off when they are feeling less confident is also good for their security.

When those with auditory in the security zone get insecure and shift into the out-of-balance qualities of the auditory, it is important to remember that they often function in extremes. Sensitivity and diplomacy go out the window. They can get angry like an erupting volcano, blurting out words with machine-gun intensity, or they may take the opposite extreme and give the silent treatment or do a disappearing act, either emotionally or physically. This only happens when they are feeling insecure; otherwise, this behaviour is not apparent. This extreme behaviour, because it is not their norm, can seem like it is coming from out of nowhere and can be confusing to those around them.

Intensity increases, as does the volume of voice, often taking on a negative tone. When insecure, these individuals are not interested in what the other person is saying, only in being heard and understood themselves. They may say aggressive things they later have no recollection of saying, and they truly don't remember.

One of the quirky things about those with auditory in the security zone is that they are hypersensitive to how others are talking to them in voice, tone, and volume, but they don't hear their own voice, tone, and volume. They may out-shout the other person, or they may just shut out the other person. At this point, it is best to give them space. When they are like this, they can dish out pressure but cannot handle being pressured back. So arguing with them will only make things worse. They will not hear you when they are like this. Give them space to calm down.

When these individuals are feeling less confident and mildly insecure, they usually exhibit aggression, impatience, frustration, and blame. If this is not being expressed outwardly, they may be imploding into themselves with negative spiral thinking instead. They have a natural ability to come up with ideas, but when this becomes negative and they turn it in on themselves, their compulsive thinking spirals out of control, causing anger, fear, depression, or stomach upset.

Repetition may become predominant, but they don't think they are being repetitive. When they are repeating, they are doing something different with the statement inside their own head, even though to you it sounds the same.

It is important for those with auditory in the security zone to have a healthy outlet for releasing the build-up of physical auditory energy. Being physically active, accomplishing things, getting the facts, understanding the situation, and keeping their finances in order will help them get back in balance and feel secure.

Ways to Create Balance

- Get active and challenge yourself.
- Get physical exercise. Sweat at least three times a week—more is better.
- Engage in physical activities with a sound component (for example, squash or tennis).
- Get the facts.
- Pursue understanding.
- Create attainable goals that you can achieve daily.
- Channel creative ideas into positive projects.
- Create or find a job where you are paid what you are worth.
- Manage your finances well.
- Have a nest egg for emergencies.
- Get your financial records in good order.
- Get rid of useless junk or worn-out stuff.

Part Six
Engaging and Bridging

Whether you are wooing a partner, teaching different processing styles, or creating a business deal, learning to engage and bridge the different processing styles is a must. Creating rapport is one of the most fundamental skills we can learn when it comes to communication.

Why would you want to know how to create rapport with people? Rapport is described as the experience of being understood without judgment—of being comfortable with another person. So momentarily, you are stepping into someone's world view or model of the world to allow communication and understanding to happen.

Because rapport builds trust, removes resistance, secures another's attention, and creates a belief that you have a knowledge, expertise, and interest, it allows you to build a connection with another person. People are more comfortable and willing to listen to people who are like them.

Rapport is a process of responsiveness, not necessarily "liking". When people are like someone, there is a kinship, and they are more willing to assist that person, more patient, and more open to communication. Rapport is about gaining someone's attention and respect for your expertise as a communicator in whatever context you are operating, professionally and/or personally.

Chapter 21
The PEP Personality Process in Relationships

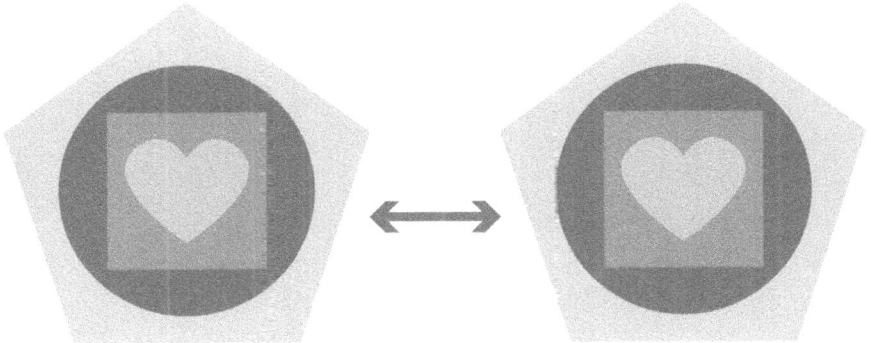

In primary relationships, it is important for each of you to know and understand your own and your partner's PEP Personality Process. After reading the information in this book, discuss how your perspectives on each other have changed. Locate areas of the relationship where you can see that issues might arise, and discuss ahead of time how you might handle them differently now that you know more about each other.

Commit to working towards acceptance or at least tolerance and a sense of humour around your differences or those areas that could potentially be troublesome. When you have a thorough understanding of how each of you process, work at meeting each other's love strategies to solidify the relationship.

Below are some of the ways that the different components in the communication zone work when it comes to love styles—that is, how those with these components view love, how they show love, and how they like to be shown love. Remember that we are only taking one aspect of a person's processing style into consideration here, and the challenge zone would come into play here as well. Eventually, we really need to take the whole PEP Personality Process into account, and this is a place to start.

A question I am often asked is, "Which combination of processing styles make for the best relationship?" My answer is simple: All processing styles can have a relationship with each other. Some are just more work than others. Meeting your partner's love strategy helps your partner to feel secure in the relationship.

A Quick Reference for the Four Love Styles

1. People with kinesthetic in the communication zone will want you to
   - provide affection and affirmation
   - offer acknowledgement and reassurance
   - engage in touching, cuddling, holding hands, and sharing
   - share stories, listen, and be interested in their life
   - make them feel cared for
   - support them emotionally
   - have fun and laugh with them
   - spend time doing things and being social together

2. People with visual in their communication zone like their partner to
   - look deeply and lovingly into their eyes
   - show caring
   - give gifts or written notes
   - be seen with them out and about
   - take their wants and needs into consideration
   - let them know they are attractive and that the partner is attracted to them
   - give recognition for who they are and what they have done
   - be on time
   - be romantic

3. People with cognitive in their communication zone will want you to
   - say the words "I love you"
   - have interesting conversations with them
   - enjoy good food with them
   - engage in sensuality, massages, foot rubs, and flirtation with them

- have a good and satisfying sexual relationship
- respect them, be honest, and have integrity
- let them know what you are up to and doing
- say what you mean and mean what you say

4. People with auditory in the communication zone will want you to

- listen to them
- do practical things together
- share ideas
- use nicknames
- do things for them
- appreciate them for doing things for you
- be physically active together (biking, swimming, tennis, etc.)
- tell them convincingly that you love them (not so much the words, but the voice, tone, tempo, and intensity)

This is only a place to start. Please feel free to explore and have fun with this. As you meet each other's love strategies, you will notice more and more that your relationship feels safer and more secure. This builds trust in the relationship.

Utilize the Language of Your Loved Ones and Those Close to You

By utilizing the language of your loved ones, you can create more rapport and a stronger connection with those you care about. Learning and applying the language of those closest to you can improve your communication with them substantially. This is because their language better fits their neurology and assists them in understanding the communication more clearly. So comprehending the language of your partner, spouse, child, or friend and learning to use their words to describe things will be beneficial.

Let's take a look at the language of the different communication styles. Bridging from your language to theirs helps them to get, see, understand, and hear you better.

Kinesthetic in the Communication Zone

If people close to you have this combination, listen to their stories and ask questions. When talking to them, use a slower and more considerate tone with some enthusiasm. Make sure you give them reassurances and good news first because this allows them to hear the rest of your points. Using their language assists them in understanding what you are saying. When you use their language, it fits for them and is more comfortable. When they are describing or communicating, they will often use long complicated sentences or stories with extensive detail; they want to give you a feeling for what they are talking about. Be patient and enjoy their stories.

Remember that all action words, emotional words, and tactile words or phrases are in the kinesthetic language category. Some examples are:

Emotions
- afraid
- aggravated
- agitated
- angry
- annoyed
- anxious
- bashful
- bored
- calm
- cherish
- depressed
- distressed
- enthusiastic
- envy
- excited
- fear
- frustrated
- glad
- gloomy
- guilt
- happy
- hateful
- heartfelt
- hope
- hurt
- joy
- love
- passionate
- sad
- shame
- sympathetic
- upset

Tactile
- alert
- alive
- balance
- blow
- breathless
- bumpy
- catch
- close
- cold
- comfortable
- concrete
- connect
- contact
- deep
- distance
- endurance
- energy
- faint
- feel
- firm
- fit
- full
- grasp
- handle
- hard
- heavy
- hungry
- light
- numb
- over
- press
- pulsing
- quick
- quiver
- rough
- rub
- scrape
- sensory
- shallow
- sharp
- slow
- smooth
- soft
- solid

- stand
- stir
- strike
- strong
- support
- throb
- tingle
- touch
- tremble
- under
- unmoving
- warm
- weak
- anything to do with tactile or the physicality of something or someone

Action
- absorbing
- acting
- affection
- busy
- caring
- comforting
- courageous
- daring
- eagerness
- emotional
- encouraged
- entertaining
- exercise
- flowing
- fun
- impression
- jump
- kind
- leap
- lively
- manipulative
- movement
- panting
- playful
- playing
- pleasure
- practice
- readiness
- running
- sensitivity
- spread
- suffer
- sulky
- surprised
- swimming
- tenderness
- tense
- thankful
- thrill
- underhanded
- unfeeling
- walking
- zeal
- all actions and action words

Phrases
- all washed up
- bite off more than you can chew
- blow off steam
- boils down to
- catch on
- chip off the old block
- come to grips with
- connect with
- control yourself
- cool, calm, and collected
- don't spread yourself too thin
- finger on the pulse
- fire it up
- firm foundation
- get a handle on
- get a hold of
- get a load of this
- get the drift of
- go-getter
- hand in hand
- hang in there
- hold it
- hold on
- keep your shirt on
- know the ropes
- lay the cards on the table
- moment of panic
- moved by
- on one's toes
- on the go
- on the rocks
- pain-in-the-neck
- pass over
- pitch in
- pull some strings
- put your best foot forward

- rubs me the wrong way
- sharp as a tack
- slip through
- smooth operator
- start from scratch
- stiff upper lip
- tap into
- topsy-turvy
- touch base
- touch upon
- turn around
- walk through

Here are couple of examples of how you might use these words:

- "I really *enjoyed* the *laughter* we *shared* and the *walk* we went on."
- "If this *feels right* for you, maybe we could *stay connected* by *holding hands* while we talk through this *distressing* topic."

Remember, the most important questions for the person with kinesthetic in the communication zone are *why* questions. Knowing why they are doing something gives them the feeling and direction they need and the motivation to do it. Asking why they are feeling a certain way can assist them in finding out valid information and shows them you care.

Visual in the Communication Zone

If people close to you have this combination, speed up when you are talking to them. Use a slightly faster pace and be excited about the topic or communication. You are going to want to paint a picture with your words. Using their language helps them get a clearer perspective on what you are talking about. It also helps them form a picture and be more willing to envision what you are saying.

Those with visual in the communication zone will use quickly grouped words with a minimum of detail when talking, describing, or communicating. They assume that you have the same picture or movie that they have. The more excited they are, the faster they will talk.

Remember that all descriptive words, colours, and external or internal visually sensed words or phrases are in the visual language category. Some examples are:

About the eyes
- 3-D
- blind
- eyesight

- far-sighted
- nearsighted
- sight
- vision

Descriptive internal visual
- brilliance
- dawn

- envision
- flashy
- illuminate
- imagine
- insight
- reflect
- shining
- showy
- visualize

The act of sight
- appear
- focus
- gaze
- glance
- glimpse
- illustrate
- imagine
- look
- observe
- peep
- picture
- reveal
- scan
- see
- show
- squint
- stare
- survey
- view
- watch

Quality of the picture
- bright
- clear
- coloured
- colourful
- colourless
- contrast
- dark
- dim
- dull
- faded
- focused
- foggy
- framed
- gleam
- glisten
- glitter
- hazy
- hue
- iridescence
- light
- pale
- panoramic
- shade
- sparkling
- tint
- tunnel vision
- twinkle
- un-faded
- unframed
- vivid

Descriptive external visual
- beam
- display
- dreamer
- flash
- glow
- illustrate
- image
- mirage
- moonlight
- movie
- outlook
- reflection
- scene
- splendour
- sunlight
- viewpoint
- vista

All colours
- beige
- black
- blue
- bronze
- brown
- gold
- green
- grey
- orange
- pink
- purple
- red
- silver
- violet
- white
- yellow
- other shades of colour, such as light blue, dark blue, indigo, turquoise

Phrases
- a look-see
- a shade of
- all the colours of the rainbow

- an eyeful
- appears to me
- at first sight
- baby blue
- beyond a shadow of a doubt
- bird's eye view
- canary yellow
- catch a glimpse of
- clear cut
- crystal clear
- dim view
- eagle eye
- eye to eye
- field of view
- flashed on
- get a perspective on
- get a scope of
- get the picture
- hazy idea
- horse of a different colour
- in light of
- in the dark
- in the green
- in the pink
- in view of
- make a scene
- mental image
- mental picture
- mind's eye
- naked eye
- paint a picture
- paint the town red
- photographic memory
- picture this
- plainly seen
- point of view
- pretty as a picture
- royal purple
- see at a glance
- see to it
- see you around
- seeing red
- short-sighted
- showing off
- sight for sore eyes
- staring off into space
- take a gander at
- take a peek
- that's clear to me
- the long view
- tunnel vision
- wall-eyes
- well defined

Here are couple of examples of how you might use these words:

- "Can you *imagine* being on that *beautiful* beach and the *bright blue* water that we'll *see* when we go to Bora Bora next month?"
- "When I *look* at you I can't *imagine* anyone else but you in my *dreams* or my life!"

Remember, the most important questions for those with visual in the communication zone are *when* questions, because they always wants to know the timing of things. When would you like to meet again? When is the deadline? When will that be complete? When is that available? When is that due? When can we arrange that? When are we getting together again? A *when* question allows them to get things organized in their timeline so they can plan for it. When you ask them these questions, it allows them to plan with you and look forward to times in the future when you will be together or doing fun things, and this will cause them to feel cared for by you.

Cognitive in the Communication Zone

If people close to you have this combination, be okay with them asking you questions. They are doing that because they care and are interested in what you are doing. One of the ways they show love is to want to be "in the know" about what you are up to.

When talking to someone with cognitive in the communication zone, use a thoughtful and considerate tone of voice. Putting what you are saying in a logical sequence and order and using cognitive language can help them to better understand what you are saying and form a conclusion. Even saying *first this, second this* can be helpful. Being as reasonable and logical as you can is helpful as well. These individuals may talk to themselves out loud quite often, and this is something to realize and accept about them. If they are not giving you much feedback, ask a question to engage them or ask their opinion—but be prepared. If you do ask their opinion, they will give it to you.

At times, they may not give an indication of understanding unless you ask them a question, because they are in information-gathering mode. Remember that all dates, numbers and data, and everything having to do with mental processes, are in the cognitive language category. Some examples of cognitive words and phrases are:

Mental processing words
- analyse
- assumption
- awareness
- believe
- comprehend
- conceive
- concentration
- conclusion
- consider
- contemplate
- decide
- deduce
- digital
- enlightenment
- experience
- faith
- imagine
- integrity
- judgement
- know
- learn
- meaning
- meditate
- muse
- perceive
- presume
- principle
- process
- question
- realize
- reason
- recall
- reflect
- remember
- sense
- sequence
- surmise
- think
- trust
- understand
- wonder

Other cognitive words
- advice

- advise
- change
- communicate
- concept
- conscious
- conviction
- data
- declaration
- deliberate
- distinct
- educate
- exaggerate
- honesty
- idea
- infer
- information
- instruct
- intercourse
- justification
- knowledge
- language
- mediate
- message
- mind
- motivate
- opinion
- persuasion
- possible
- probable
- procedure
- rational
- report
- sequence
- teach
- unconscious
- words

All dates
- January
- February
- March
- April
- May
- June
- July
- August
- September
- October
- November
- December

All numbers or sequencing
- using either digits, *1, 2, 3*; or letters, *A, B, C*.
- also numbers spelled out, like *first*, *second*, etc.

All data
facts and statistics collected together for reference, analysis, or calculations

Phrases
- a sense of …
- be conscious of
- change is good
- consider learning …
- considering that …
- distinct possibility of …
- Does that make sense?
- I can conceive of that.
- I can experience …
- I don't know …
- I don't understand your meaning.
- I have a real knowing about that.
- I know.
- I need more information.
- I perceive that to be …
- I sense that …
- I thought …
- I understand that …
- I will consider your question.
- I wonder if …
- in that process
- inquire into
- make a decision
- make sense
- my discernment
- my idea
- reason it through
- That makes sense.
- That's a good question.

Knowing Me, Knowing You

- the conscious conception is ...
- the content included ...
- the learning process ..
- the procedures are ...
- the process is ...
- the wonder of it all
- the word on that is ...
- thinking about that
- to motivate, you can ...
- to sequence it
- understanding is ...
- without a doubt
- word for word
- You know what I mean.

Here are couple of examples of how you might use these words:

- "*Thinking* about our trip on *June 28*, I can't help but *wonder* what it will *mean* to your parents, *considering* they've been *communicating* for some time now that they want us to come for a visit."
- "Your *words* really *make sense* to me!"

Remember, the most important questions for the person with cognitive in the communication zone are *what* questions:

- What's happening?
- What's going on?
- What are we going to do about that?
- What's your opinion?
- What's that about?
- What do you want to do?
- What have we covered so far?
- What is left to do?
- What are the facts?
- What are you doing?
- What have you heard?
- What's the word on that?

They want information so they can make sense of it, understand it, or know where it fits in the bigger picture. They are information gatherers. They are constantly analysing themselves and the world around them. As a loved one, that includes you as well. Asking *what* questions lets them know you are interested in them and that you care.

Auditory in the Communication Zone

If people close to you have this combination, the best thing you can do for them is to really listen and be a sounding board for their ideas. Remember, they do not necessarily want your input, solutions, or questions. How you talk to them is almost more important than what you say. If you want to feel really heard by them, you need to talk to them in a fairly loving but firm voice. Your tone of voice is important, and if it doesn't have a certain level of intensity to it, they don't believe it. They'll dismiss your message or think it is not important. It is okay, and often preferred, to be very direct and to the point, even blunt.

Those with auditory in the communication zone like to talk and work or talk and be doing something else, and some of the best conversations with them can be had by doing this. They will often talk in bursts of speech and blurt things out, and sometimes the blurting may be inappropriate. Usually, their speech has a rhythmic quality, and they tend to use their voice (tone, tempo, and volume), sound effects, and even *ums* and *ahs* to emphasize things or give their speech life. They will often interrupt and use lots of *ums* and *ahs* as punctuation when speaking.

These individuals like talking on the phone, and sometimes you may communicate more on the phone than in person. They will let you know when they understand you or what you are saying by changing the subject. Remember that all sounds used in speech are auditory, and anything that has to do with hearing or making sound is in the auditory language category.

Some examples of auditory words and phrases are:

Articulating
- aloud
- announce
- answer
- articulation
- assertion
- belittle
- bellow
- berate
- blab
- broadcast
- chattering
- chatty
- comment
- conversation
- converse

- conversing
- cry
- cuss
- declaration
- declare
- decry
- diction
- disclosing
- discuss
- discussing
- enunciating
- explain
- express
- expressing
- expression
- gab

- gossip
- insult
- mention
- narrate
- orating
- outspoken
- proclaim
- pronouncing
- pronunciation
- ranting
- repeating
- report
- reproach
- say
- saying
- scold

- shout
- speak
- speaking
- speech
- spouting
- state
- swear
- talking
- tell
- translating
- utterance
- verbalization
- vocalization
- voicing
- whisper
- yell

Listening
- accent
- attune
- audible
- deaf
- deafen
- earful
- eavesdropping
- hear
- hearsay
- hush
- hushed
- inaudibility
- listen
- musical
- muted
- noise
- overhear
- overtones
- phonetics
- quiet
- record
- rumour
- silence
- speechless
- unhearing

Sound quality
- acoustic
- acoustics
- alto
- baritone
- bass
- cadence
- intensity
- intonation
- loudness
- pitch
- raspy
- resound
- reverberate
- reverberation
- soprano
- sound
- tempo
- tenor
- timbre
- tone
- vibration
- voice
- volume

Sound effects
- bang
- bash
- blast
- boom
- buzz
- clang
- clapping
- clatter
- click
- crack
- drumming
- echo
- explosion
- growl
- knock
- pop
- racket
- rattle
- ring
- roar
- rumble
- scraping
- screech
- shrillness
- siren
- slam
- slap
- snap
- squawking
- squeaking
- strumming
- thunder
- tinkling
- toot
- twang
- uproar
- wham
- whistle

Things that make sound
- accordion

- alphorn
- bagpipes
- banjo
- bell
- castanets
- cello
- chimes
- clarinet
- cymbals
- didgeridoo
- drum
- flute
- gong
- guitar
- harp
- horn
- marimba
- oboe
- piano
- rattle
- saxophone
- tambourine
- triangle
- trombone
- trumpet
- tuba
- ukulele
- violin
- xylophone
- zither
- any musical instrument or thing that makes sound

Phrases

- all ears
- be heard
- blabbermouth
- call on
- chatty Cathy
- clear as a bell
- clearly expressed
- describe in detail
- double-talk
- express yourself
- give an account of
- give me your ear
- grant an audience
- heard voices
- hidden message
- hold your tongue
- idle talk
- in earshot
- in full cry
- just clicked
- keynote speaker
- loud and clear
- make music
- manner of speaking
- plain-spoken
- power of speech
- purrs like a kitten
- rap session
- rat-a-tat
- rings a bell
- state your purpose
- strain of melody
- tattletale
- tell me
- to tell the truth
- tongue-tied
- tune in/tune out
- unheard of
- voice an opinion

Here are couple of examples of how you might use these words:

- "When you *whispered* to me that you loved me, everything just *clicked*."
- "That *rings a bell*; I remember when you *told* me that."

Remember, the most important questions for those with auditory in the communication zone are *where* and *what if* questions, because these help to determine the value of information and communication. They will value you more and feel understood when you ask questions like:

- Where does this fit for you?

- Where do you think ...?
- Where is it applicable?
- Where is it useful?
- What if we used this to ...?
- What if we applied it to ...?

When you ask them these types of questions, it helps them to value you more, and they feel understood by you.

If people with auditory in the communication zone determine that something is not useful, practical, or up to their quality standards, they will throw it out, dismiss it, or give it little to no value. If you can tell them how something is useful, practical, or of value, this helps them understand what you are saying.

Chapter 22
The PEP Personality Process in Teaching, Facilitating, and Learning

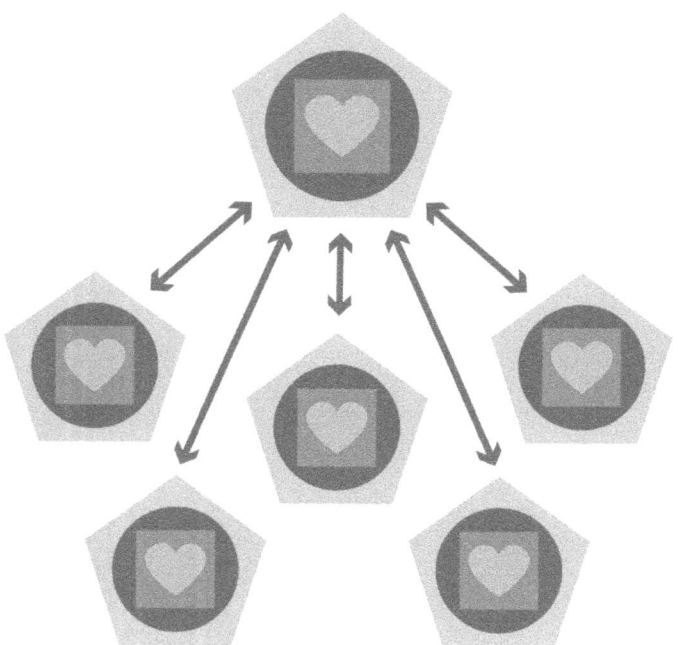

To engage all participants when you're facilitating a group, make sure that you're teaching to all four styles of learning based on the four different components in the communication zone. Remember, all people have kinesthetic, visual, auditory, and cognitive components and the personality functions of those components; they just operate through the four zones differently. Teach students utilizing all of those learning styles to provide a solid, clear, meaningful, and practical learning experience.

When setting up your lesson plan, lecture, or class session, there is a system of flow which works well for all of the learning styles. One way of doing this is to make sure you include the answers to the questions below, which are most important to each of the components in the communication zone:

- Start by answering the *what* questions. This is where you give the theories and information about what you will be teaching.
- Next, answer the *why* questions. This is where you give the feeling of motivation for learning and why it would serve the participants.
- Next, answer the *when* questions to give participants a time frame in which to organize the project or learning and the deadlines they will need to meet.
- Next, all of the PEP Personality Process styles need the *how* questions answered. The *how* part of the program and the learning itself can be given in all four styles, based on the different components in the communication zone.
- Last but definitely not least, ask the *where* and *what if* questions, which give an understanding of where the information, skill, or learning can be applied, fits, or is useful.

Components in the Environmental Zones and Learning

When teaching, facilitating, or learning, one of the most important things to be aware of is the component in the environmental zone. When teaching a class, you need to be aware of all of the components, because this is where the information interfaces with the person first from their environment, and this is how the information is then delivered to the component in the communication zone to be interpreted. For example:

- If I have kinesthetic in my environmental zone, I will want to know why we are learning or doing the exercise. It is important for me to

be comfortable in my environment, and if I can have a hands-on learning opportunity, that's great, too.
- If I have visual in my environmental zone, then having the information presented in a visually stimulating way will be an important part of my learning. I need a clear view of what is going on, without a lot of distractions.
- If I have cognitive in my environmental zone, having the information presented in a logical sequence or delivered in a series of steps done in a certain order is extremely useful. Also, the words you use to describe what you are talking about need to be clear and logical.
- If I have auditory in my environmental zone, having the information delivered in a clear, pleasing, firm, and modulated tone of voice, with some enthusiasm, will assist my learning. Sound effects can also help.

We must take each person's whole PEP Personality Process into account when teaching or facilitating. This is why learning to teach or facilitate in all of the four components and their personality functions is so important.

Let's look at some specific methods that will assist people who have that component in the communication zone, because this is where the information or learning is consolidated.

The Kinesthetic Learner

The learner with kinesthetic in the communication zone will benefit from the following tools and strategies:

- stories and metaphors
- acting things out
- hands-on experiences (moving, touching, and doing)
- experiments and activities
- repetition
- working in teams/pairs, connecting with the teacher/facilitator and others
- a comfortable setting
- making it a game or fun
- role-playing
- field trips

Kinesthetic learners are action-oriented, tactile, and enthusiastic. They are team players who learn best through hands-on training. They memorize and learn by methodically doing or walking through something, usually several times. Getting a feeling for what they are learning takes up more neurology, and therefore it takes more time in the beginning for the person with kinesthetic in the communication zone to get it. Once they do get it, though, they really have it. Making work fun and comfortable creates an effective learning environment for these learners.

The Visual Learner

The learner with visual in the communication zone will benefit from the following tools and strategies:

- visually appealing handouts
- diagrams, pictures, illustrations, and visual aids
- schedules, deadlines, and agendas
- colour coding and fill-in-the-blanks worksheets
- the ability to see the teacher or facilitator in person or online
- PowerPoint slides
- demonstrations/models

Visual learners grasp concepts quickly and can get bored easily if they don't have any visual stimulation or there is too much detail. They are highly intellectual and perceptive, and learning is often fun for them.

Visual learners enjoy and benefit from using visual aids: pictures, illustrations, written instructions, agendas, demonstrations, and models. When they read information, they create an internal picture or movie which they can quickly recall when needed. Some visual learners, because they memorize by seeing pictures or the written word, can see things just once and have that information available. Others have a complete photographic memory.

The Cognitive Learner

The learner with cognitive in the communication zone will benefit from the following tools and strategies:

- discussions or question periods
- debates

- lectures
- books
- information given in a logical, sequential way or in a series of logical steps
- appropriate data such as percentages, statistics, numbers, and dates
- theories and how they connect to the future or bigger picture

People with cognitive in the communication zone learn by memorizing steps, procedures, and sequences. They will want to know if something "makes sense". They are constantly going in and out of a light trance. This occurs because they are going from gathering information in the outside world to fitting it in and making sense of it according to what they already know in their internal world. They may be re-evaluating or expanding on what is already known. In order to understand an event or communication, they must make reasonable, logical sense of it and give it meaning.

Cognitive learners do not like education for education's sake. Although they love information, it needs to be of value to them or at least of interest to them and to fit in with their life's plan. If they are not interested in it, they will do just enough to get by.

The Auditory Learner

The learner with auditory in the communication zone will benefit from the following tools and strategies:

- delivery or presentation in a pleasing moderated voice tone, whether in person, on the phone, or through audio
- brainstorming/coming up with ideas
- understanding the information by knowing where to apply it and where it is useful
- music, musical instruments, and musical anchors or cues
- discussions/question periods
- lectures/talks
- doing something useful with the learning and applying it to a specific situation
- repeating things out loud
- listening to recordings of the lecture or talk

People with auditory in the communication zone learn by discussing things and understanding where that information is applicable. They must understand something before they can accept it. They are practical-minded and need to know where they can apply new information or skills they are learning. If they can't apply it, they don't value it.

Auditory learners can repeat things back to you easily. They learn well by listening, and programs delivered by audio are good for them. They enjoy talking on the phone, so coaching by phone, computer, or audio device may appeal to them. Auditory learners like to be told how they are doing and respond to certain tones of voice. Delivering your words with a firmness and a slightly louder tone helps them take you seriously. These learners are interested in ideas, brainstorming, and where learning will create improvements.

In Conclusion

If you are teaching in all four communication styles, you will be engaging your students on more than one level of learning. They'll have a better understanding of the material; they will retain it longer; and they will also have an enjoyable experience of learning.

Chapter 23
Utilizing the Processing Styles in Business

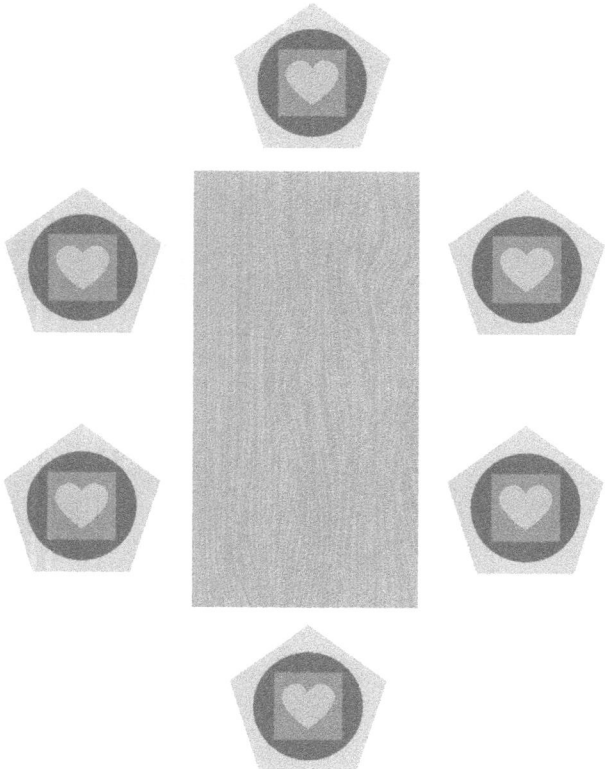

The PEP Personality Process is extremely useful in business, for engaging with co-workers and management teams; utilizing the strengths of your workers; and minimizing challenges. By understanding and learning to work with each person—using bridging and communication for the different people on your team—you will get more of a buy-in to what it is the group is working to achieve. Knowing your differences, strengths, and the areas where you may need some assistance makes for a more cohesive team.

In one of the trainings I did with a small engineering company, I worked with the team and the owner to rewrite the job descriptions for each member so that the jobs fit the person's strengths and interests while minimizing the challenges of that individual's processing style. What we found was that the team was more effective and happier, and the business grew and became more successful in a very short time. With an understanding of each individual's PEP Personality Processing style of communication, acceptance of others improved, and the team in general functioned much better.

On the following pages, you will find a description of each of the components in the communication zone and how these generally operate in a business setting. Remember, this is an overview of the communication zone only, and the whole processing style of each member of your team should be taken into consideration. The information here will give you the core around which the other parts of each individual's personality operates.

Working with Kinesthetic Communicators

Generally, those with kinesthetic in the communication zone do their best as team players. Often as leaders or managers, they manage by consensus. They are good workers in general who have the ability to act and get things done. If they have enough socializing and fun on the job, they will be exceedingly motivated, hard workers. They are excellent at following instructions once they have a feeling for the project, and they are conscientious about their work. They are skilled, although sometimes challenged by organizing details.

The person who has kinesthetic in the communication zone generally responds better to physical and emotional rewards and praise because it feels good to get rewarded and singled out for a job well done. Too much harsh criticism or threats, and they may make more mistakes or have more sick days. They take everything personally. Too much conflict will cause them to quit or leave a situation.

When people who have kinesthetic in the communication zone are happy on the job, they are willing and easy to work with and genuinely help-oriented, for they are people-people. They have a natural affinity and caring for others. If they are enthusiastic about a project, they can create enthusiasm in everyone around them.

When working with people who have kinesthetic in the communication zone, remember that these individuals actually need to be social and have time during the workday to interact with others. Building good relationships on the job keeps them happy and more productive. When interacting with kinesthetic communicators, it is important to show genuine interest in them as a person as well as an employee. Take the time to get to know them and be sensitive to their needs. They are emotionally based people who are compassionate, nurturing, sensitive, and fun-loving. Help them to be comfortable on the job and you will have a loyal and hardworking team player.

Boundaries are a challenge for those with kinesthetic in the communication zone, so it is important to give these individuals time and space to make the right decision. If you push them to give you an answer right away, they will often give you the answer you want simply because they don't like conflict. Afterwards, they will either look like they are changing their mind or they will do what they agreed to and then resent you—or they may just avoid doing what they said they would do. Because they may have difficulty setting appropriate boundaries, they can also become too involved or sympathetic to other people's needs, issues, or problems.

There are times when people who are kinesthetic communicators can go out of balance or off their pivot, and they can react by becoming childish. Or they can go into the kinesthetic wallow, which means going into a negative emotion and wallowing around in it. They can become irrational at times like this because feelings are not necessarily rational or logical.

They work best when you provide a detailed or specific plan to be accomplished. So make sure you clearly define the goals for them and provide ongoing support where needed. The people who are kinesthetic communicators truly love to be recognized and appreciated for their achievements, accomplishments, and goals, because they respond much better to the carrot than the stick (reward vs. punishment). In fact, the stick approach will fail miserably.

When presenting new ideas, do so with thoughtful consideration. Slow down the process and answer questions as patiently and thoroughly as possible. If you can, make things fun, personable, and friendly. These individuals don't like long, boring explanations with too much data; they have a more hands-on approach and want to move into action.

In general, those with kinesthetic in the communication zone are optimistic, outgoing, and action-oriented. If they can make a task fun, they will. They work well with teams and sharing tasks, thoughts, and ideas. They encourage informality, as this is more comfortable for them. They have a natural ability to relate to others and great people skills. They prefer to take an experiential approach to everything they do. They can be outspoken, enthusiastic, and stimulating, which can enliven a group or team.

Why questions are important to these workers, so make sure they know why they are doing what they are doing. They are attracted to new challenges and experiences and commonly act on gut feelings rather than logical analysis. They are quick to move into action, which is useful in roles requiring action and initiative. They have a strong tendency to adapt to people and surroundings in order to promote harmony and comfort. They are consistent, reliable performers who seek help from others when they need it.

These individuals have a tendency to avoid change and conflict, so you need to give them time to adjust to change. They like it when you get excited about things and show them positive emotions. They dislike it when they are treated impersonally or ignored. They like to be treated with respect and in a friendly, personal manner.

The businessperson who is kinesthetic in the communication zone has the following advantages, challenges, and needs.

Advantages	*Challenges*	*Needs*
• great social and people skills	• takes things too personally	• friendliness
• team player	• can be too social or chatty	• sincere appreciation
• action oriented	• personal life can interfere with professional life	
• good with details	• misery loves company (when out of balance)	

Working with Visual Communicators

People with visual in the communication zone are known for their high standards, efficiency, and impeccability when it comes to their work. These are the visionaries, the ones who want everything to run smoothly and to be and do their best. They grasp the big picture and all of the facets of a project quickly. They often even pick up on details missed by others.

Visual communicators are generally organized, neat, and tidy in their work environment and expect this in others. They need to be organized, with their priorities in place, so that they can stay on track and not be overwhelmed by the tasks at hand. They often prefer to do business in person, especially at first, so that they can see others' responses first-hand.

Visual communicators have an ability second to none to plan and organize projects, events, and timing—if they have the overall picture. They have an incredible talent for being able to see the finished or completed project and know what it will look like because of their natural skill for visualizing. They carry this vision clearly in their mind, and that gives them the ability to present the plan and guide others. Being recognized and acknowledged for their work is important. Praise, appreciation, and recognition in a visible way will keep them motivated to do their best.

When working with the person who has visual in the communication zone, remember that visual communicators are quick learners. They pick things up faster than other styles and can get bored if things go on too long. They are organizers, planners, and intellectuals, and they are goal-oriented. They need to have things planned in advance and want to know the timing and deadlines on every project. They are self-disciplined and self-motivated, and they will naturally spend endless hours in deep concentration. They like helping and supporting others. Harmony is important to them.

Visual communicators want to be recognized for their achievements and accomplishments. They like it when you are supportive and show you care. They respond well to and appreciate applause, recognition, and positive feedback. They like positive attention but dislike wasting time or getting negative feedback. Time is a commodity they hold dear, and if you need to give them negative feedback, make sure you do it in private, out of earshot of anyone else. They can dish out criticism but do not handle criticism from others well.

They play by the rules and expect others to also play by the rules, and they prefer that the rules be clearly defined. When they get into a competitive situation, they really like to win. They like to be efficient and get things done quickly—preferably now. They work best when they have a clear goal they can picture or a reward that they are working towards.

Visual communicators appear quiet and reserved until you get to know them. They are charismatic people who have a great deal of enthusiasm for whatever they are involved in and seek perfection in everything that they do. They are often described as intelligent, careful, exacting, neat, organized, systematic, accurate, and tactful. They are concerned, cautious, and correct.

These individuals are often focused on the details and quality they are producing. They plan ahead, make lists, and are constantly checking for accuracy. They are consistent and reliable, and they like stability. The visual communicator's challenges are flexibility and perfectionism. They try to avoid mistakes and can get caught in a fixed picture of how it should be according to the picture in their head.

When these individuals go out of balance, they react to pressure by becoming silent, withdrawn, and introspective. They can put others under time pressure—and when under pressure themselves, they can be quite verbally cutting. They can be stubborn when others are trying to introduce a new way of doing something if it doesn't fit their picture.

When introducing a new way of doing something or a change to procedure or schedule, expect resistance and make sure you give these individuals some time to change the picture. It is better to say you do not know something than to say "maybe" or "it's a possibility," for once visual communicators form a picture in their head, they expect you to deliver. Only give them a timeframe if you know you are going to meet it.

The business person with visual in the communication zone has the following advantages, challenges, and needs:

Advantages	Challenges	Needs
• organized	• time pressure	• admiration
• planning ability	• too exacting	• recognition
• skill with timelines and deadlines	• inflexible	
• good at setting goals	• must be able to do it perfectly the first time or chooses not to try	
	• lack of patience with others	

Working with Cognitive Communicators

People with cognitive in the communication zone plan ahead and can carry projected programs through to completion. They command respect and are highly intuitive and productive. These individuals usually grasp the overall picture quickly, and that includes all the important details. They excel as executives and managers with their ability to size things up quickly and weigh options.

The person with cognitive in the communication zone works well with most processing styles and has innate skills when it comes to managing people and projects. Diplomacy is this individual's middle name when it comes to handling people and events. Words and the use of words, both spoken and written, come easily to cognitive communicators. They have an innate ability to find and seek the connections and interrelatedness behind most things.

Workers with cognitive in the communication zone are extremely solution-focused and love to problem-solve and analyse. They have high integrity on the job and in everything they do, and they value this in others. They take a great deal of pride in being fair-minded, reasonable, and objective. Often, they can remain level-headed even when others are upset.

Cognitive communicators like systems, routines, and order. They have a high need for information and often will do a lot of research into whatever they are doing. They can be extremely singularly focused when on a project and like it when they meet the end objective.

When working with people with cognitive in the communication zone, remember that they are disciplined, committed, responsible, creative people who prize individuality and autonomy. They are orderly, rational, logical thinkers who are analysing and making sense of everything and everyone around them. In their youth, they typically possessed a quality of being "wise beyond their years." They are known for being unusually deep thinkers, always searching for truth and meaning and wanting to make sense of the world around them.

Generally, these individuals are seen as serious, aloof, decisive, and direct, with a strong sense of realism. They talk in conclusions, ask questions, and want to be "in the know" about things. They are intellectually sharp and unusually creative. They want people when they want them and don't want them when they don't. They crave privacy and a place to be alone to get the work done.

Because of their understanding and ability with words, cognitive communicators are natural mediators who can resolve disputes quickly and effectively. They are excellent at negotiations. They quickly grasp the situation and are extremely solution-oriented. They excel at understanding a wide range of information—conceptual, innovative, and theoretical—and are good at organizing it into a clear, logical sequence and format.

People with cognitive in the communication zone are empathetic and cooperative, and they are usually good and supportive managers. They are totally comfortable in the world of their mind, and they often prefer their own thoughts to a superficial dialogue with others. They are strong-willed and have enormous willpower, as well as a tremendous capacity for endurance and seeing things through to completion. They seek the pertinent data and information, ask many questions, and behave methodically and systematically.

These individuals love being right, and once they have come to a conclusion about something, unless you can give them logical reasonable information which would cause them to re-evaluate that conclusion, they will debate the rightness of their conclusion with you. They dislike being unprepared or surprised by things and can react to pressure by taking charge or taking more control of a situation.

Cognitive communicators like it when things make sense and the reasoning and logic are solid. They appreciate activities that lead to results. They need to be in charge of their own destiny and make their own decisions.

They really dislike being wrong or making an error. They definitely work best with a structure or a framework. Often, they are seen as calm, relaxed, patient, predictable, deliberate, stable, and consistent, with a tendency to not show their feelings or share much personally. *What* questions are important to them; they want to be "in the know."

When working with cognitive communicators, warn them in advance and avoid surprises, as they do not like things being sprung on them. Be as prepared as possible. Don't ad-lib—they will see right through it. Where possible, be as logical, accurate and clear with data as you can. Show how things fit into the bigger picture and where you are going with it. Asking for their opinion will get you useful information. They prefer not to be interrupted in their work. Treat them with respect, and they will return the favour.

The businessperson with cognitive in the communication zone has the following advantages, challenges, and needs:

Advantages	*Challenges*	*Needs*
• management/research abilities	• having too singular a focus	• trust
• talent for finding the connections and interrelatedness behind most things	• forgetting to share information	• respect
• skill at problem-solving and analysing	• thinking too much about the future and not always present	• integrity
• ability to logically sequence and order information, projects, and priorities	• being a know-it-all when they are out of balance	• information
	• seeming intimidating to others	

Working with Auditory Communicators

People with auditory in the communication zone tend to demand the lead position. They are real go-getters and often are pioneers and innovators in their field of expertise. They are spearheads: they like to go in and shake things up, start new projects, or get the show on the road. They may delegate the actual work to others, for they are good at delegation, but they see themselves as the catalyst that gets things moving.

Auditory communicators can have many ideas or projects going on at once and find it easy to bounce back and forth between them. They may not, at times, be the most diplomatic leaders, but they are certainly the most intense ones. They bring their energy into the room, and you know they are going to crack the whip. They are achievement-driven and work best in autonomy.

These individuals have a deep and genuine love for their fellow humans and the world, which comes out in their high need for fairness. They expect that others will need only the facts and the end goal and will work independently without much supervision or instruction. This is how they like to work themselves, and they feel it would be insulting to others to tell them how it should be done. They can at times be surprised or irritated when they find others need more information or how-to.

Auditory communicators can get along well with people and be good leaders because they value self-respect, respect for others, and free will. They trust that others can and will do their part. They have a strong sense of inner authority and find it easy to delegate and direct.

When working with the person with auditory in the communication zone, you will find that these individuals are intense, serious, determined, bold, aggressive, competitive, forceful, outspoken, productive, and full of ideas. Natural-born leaders, they can dish out pressure but do not take it well. They are strong, type-A personalities who are ambitious and want to be at the top in their chosen fields. They are easily bored, have high vitality and energy, and seek out stimulation by stirring things up and getting things going. Then they are off to the next project.

If they have too much work or not enough variety or are not being compensated fairly, they can become angry or depressed. Consumed with where they are going, they can be oblivious to other people's feelings. They are quick to become frustrated and like to have their own way. Their opinions are decisive and strong, and they are insulted when anyone tells them how to do anything. They react to pressure in extremes by either becoming argumentative and loud or giving the silent treatment.

These individuals really like it when they can share their ideas because they have creative minds that are constantly coming up with new concepts. They like to experiment with their innovations and stimulate others. They are good at finding practical uses for their ideas and theories.

They like challenges and are driven to accomplish things. Direct, to the point, and bottom-line oriented, they have a tendency to be blunt sometimes, even rude. They are decisive and work best when you allow them the freedom to do things their own way.

Auditory communicators are often described as demanding, forceful, and aggressive. They use their minds to find solutions to practical issues and are pioneering, inventive, productive, independent, and strong-willed. They enjoy challenges, taking action, and getting results, and they tend to tell or order people rather than ask. With diplomacy as their main challenge, they aren't known for their people skills.

The questions most important to auditory communicators are of the *where to apply it?* or *how to apply it?* variety. When dealing with these individuals, be factual, focused, and to the point. Talking about how potential problems could hinder accomplishments spurs the auditory communicator to brainstorm practical solutions.

The businessperson with auditory in the communication zone has the following advantages, challenges, and needs:

Advantages	*Challenges*	*Needs*
• ability to brainstorm and generate ideas	• lack of diplomacy	• respect
• talent for getting the show on the road	• too dictatorial	• results
• innovative thinking	• not organized enough	
• practical thinking	• too intense	
• insight for improvement	• bullies when out of balance	

Chapter 24
Processing Styles in Selling and Marketing

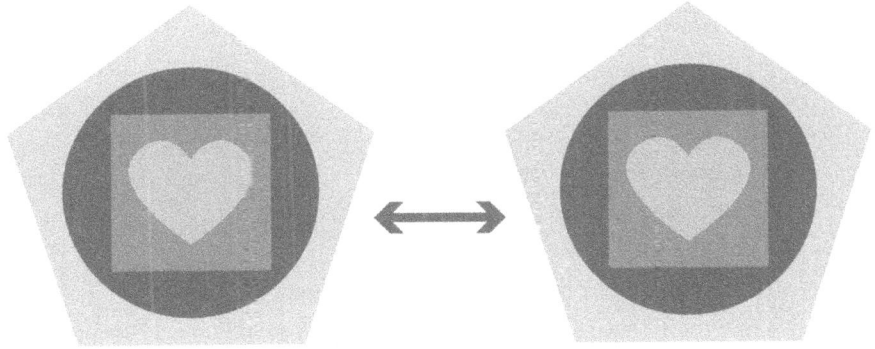

When marketing or selling, it is important to know who your market is and who you are selling to. How you phrase your promotions or brochures and even your business cards can play a part in attracting or putting off your clientele.

For instance, a commercial comes to mind of a large truck manufacturer who showed a video of a busy intersection and stated, "This is a human brain." Right away, a cognitive communicator would think, *No it isn't*. Then, the commercial showed a mountaintop, and the advertising said, "This is a speed bump." Again, the cognitive communicator would think, *No it isn't*. By the end of the commercial, when it proclaims that this is the best truck, you can probably see that all the ad has done is set up a response of *No it isn't* for the cognitive communicator.

On the other hand, I have seen toilet paper ads with two fluffy kittens playing with the toilet roll, and they are so cute and fluffy. This would be totally appealing to kinesthetic communicators. Then you have the auditory jingles on TV or the radio, which if done well can really stick with auditory communicators (or if done badly, may turn them off your product forever). You can include all of the components in your advertising, or you can target different processing styles by doing selective marketing. The key is to know who you are marketing to.

Once you have attracted the customer, it is important to pay attention to the particular component and discover how the individual is communicating so that you can use the appropriate language and give the person what is needed to make a decision.

In One-on-One Sales

To sell to people with kinesthetic in the communication zone:

- Use their language and meet their speed of conversation.
- Ask questions and listen attentively.
- Be enthusiastic and friendly.
- Take the time to establish good will.
- Let them hold or do a demo of the product.
- Give them testimonials or stories of other satisfied customers.

To sell to people with visual in the communication zone:

- Use their language and meet their speed of conversation.
- Be excited.
- Show them the product.
- Be professional.
- Be organized.
- Offer personal assurances and support.
- Be patient.
- Avoid any criticism.

To sell to people with cognitive in the communication zone:

- Use their language and meet their speed of conversation.
- Give them logical information.
- Help them meet their objectives.
- Be prompt and organized.
- Use a no-nonsense, businesslike approach.

- Show proof and documentation.
- Never pressure them to make a quick decision.

To sell to people with auditory in the communication zone:

- Use their language and meet their speed of conversation.
- Be businesslike.
- Be efficient and to the point.
- Use facts and figures.
- Ask specific questions related to the key issues.
- Tell them how this product has improved or is on the leading edge

Effective Marketing

Kinesthetic

People with kinesthetic in the communication zone respond to marketing that invokes a feeling and promotions that have testimonials of other satisfied customers. For example: "Feel the excitement and fun that driving a new Toyota Prius brings. Come in and test drive this environmentally friendly car today!"

Visual

People with visual in the communication zone need to have good-quality pictures and visuals as well as well-organized information. For example: "Imagine yourself driving a new Toyota Prius, showing people you care about the environment. Come in and see it for yourself today!" accompanied by a quality picture.

Cognitive

People with cognitive in the communication zone respond to marketing that makes sense, and information is key here. Always be able to back up your claims with real factual information and data. For example: "It makes sense to drive this environmentally smart, cost-efficient Toyota Prius! Come in today for the stats and data on this car!"

Auditory

People with auditory in the communication zone need marketing that lets them know how cutting-edge your product is. Use music or sounds that fit and jingles that stick. For example: "Have you heard the new Toyota Prius has arrived? The car hardly makes a sound, but the leading-edge technology speaks volumes! Come in and ask us about it today!"

Combination Marketing

To ring in a wide range of customers, do a combination of things that appeal to most if not all of the processing styles. For example: "Looking for comfort, quality, and cost-effective transportation? Driving a Toyota Prius gives you all that and means you care about the environment too! This is a car that takes you from where you are and into the future! Ask for a test drive today and feel the difference!"

Do this with a quality photo or video, and if it's on TV or the internet, do it with appealing music of the generation you are selling to. If you have a quality jingle, you could use that. Just make sure it's a good one.

Conclusion

This book is intended to introduce you to the PEP Personality Process as a new model and to help you understand how to work with it. It is a starting place for understanding the different zones that we naturally move in and out of and the components that each of us have—and which work differently depending on which zone they are in.

> *The better you know yourself, the better your relationship*
> *with the rest of the world.*—Toni Collette

Knowing ourselves helps us to be less needy and more confident, more effective, and more responsible for our choices in life. Self-knowledge helps us have more meaningful lives and set goals we are passionate about. In truly knowing ourselves, we know what to do to when we are out of balance and how to move back into it. We recognize when our behaviour is not our best and have the tools and skills to bring ourselves back into top form.

Knowing our strengths, our weaker areas, our natural talents, and our challenges assists us in accepting ourselves more and gives us the ability to accept and acknowledge others for who they are. We as human beings have a tendency to project our "stuff"—that is, our issues and challenges—onto others. This is often because we are unaware of our own tendencies and do not know ourselves. As the quote above suggests, as we get to know ourselves better, we have better relationships with others and the world.

Knowing ourselves matters, because the more we really understand what makes us tick, the more aware we are, and the more we have the ability to change the things we want to change and enhance the things we want more of.

> *Every human has four endowments—self-awareness, conscience, independent will and creative imagination. These give us the ultimate human freedom ... The power to choose, to respond, to change.*—Stephen Covey

One of the main reasons I wrote this book was to assist people in really having that self-awareness. I believe that when we know ourselves and take responsibility for and acknowledge who we are, we are more accepting and compassionate—not only with ourselves but in building more meaningful and beneficial relationships with others.

> *Trust is the glue of life. It's the most essential ingredient in effective communication. It's the foundational principle that holds all relationships.*—Stephen Covey

This brings me to the second reason I wrote this book: better communication. If you are looking for a magic skill to get you through life with greater ease and success, communicating well is it. Communication at its simplest involves a sender communicating a thought, feeling, or need and a receiver being able to interpret and understand that thought, feeling, or need.

Most conflict is the result of a misunderstanding in communication or a misinterpretation of a communication given verbally or in writing. Becoming effective at bridging the communication gaps, resolving conflicts, and being flexible in your ability to use the communication styles and language allows you to create a more harmonious environment. This increases happiness, because you are reducing conflict.

Effective communication can decrease verbal altercations and assist in managing anger, and it allows you to express yourself and be understood. Being a great communicator boosts your confidence and self-esteem and makes you more charismatic, which builds better relationships. Communication connects you with others. It builds friendships, attracts partners, keeps you in the loop with your children, helps with better teamwork at the office, and shows people love and respect, which leads to trust. As Stephen Covey asserts, "Trust is the glue of life."

Understanding how to effectively communicate with others can reduce your stress and increase your success in your personal and professional life.

Good communication promotes an understanding both of self and of others. People will be more likely to assist you and listen to you, and they may even like you more.

In the workplace, better communication and understanding of processing styles promotes and encourages increased productivity and job satisfaction, better feedback, less misunderstandings, quality work, the smooth communication of ideas, improved teamwork, more effective problem-solving, and fewer sick days.

> *Feelings of worth can flourish only in an atmosphere where individual differences are appreciated, mistakes are tolerated, communication is open, and rules are flexible—the kind of atmosphere that is found in a nurturing family.—Virginia Satir*

We are not all the same. In addition to the twenty-four different PEP Personality Processing styles, there are different cultures, different religions, different interests, different values, and even different sexes. Knowing who we are and learning to know who others are, as well as gaining an understanding and appreciation of our differences, is crucial.

Valuing and accepting our differences works so much more effectively than trying to impose a one-size-fits-all approach—or worse, judging as wrong anything or anyone who is different or does things differently than us. We all have our own filters, and we tend as human beings to run everything through these as we interpret the world. We need to start understanding that our differences are a positive thing and that other people do things for different reasons—and to stop interpreting everything only through the narrow view of our own filters.

Our differences give us a richness, a creativity, that can broaden our horizons. Our diversity can illuminate different ways of doing things, allow for innovations and new insights, and help us grow and enrich our lives. As we learn to accept our differences and allow people to be who they are instead of trying to change them to be more like us, and as we learn to work collaboratively with them by utilizing their strengths and ours together, we build stronger relationships, teams, and partnerships.

As we understand and work with each other, our perspectives are stretched and expanded. This opens doors to new opportunities and an enhanced view of the world we live in. When we accept ourselves, we create empowerment. Freedom is gained when we accept others for who they are, and happiness is a result of acknowledging that we are all worthy of respect. Our differences make us stronger, and our collaborative contributions innovate and build better, stronger organizations; more solid and trusting relationships; and diverse and growing communities that promote a more enlightened world.

We need to develop an attitude of curiosity about our differences and a respect for how we are similar and how we are different. We need to understand that differences are not a personal affront and quit taking things so personally. We need to learn to judge less and respect more, and to open to new possibilities, creativity, and change, with the understanding that *change* is a positive word and differences are a gift.

If we are starting to react or feel uncomfortable with something or someone, we need to learn to stay engaged and clarify—to understand what the facts of the situation are and to question what else could possibly be going on. Stop making assumptions, particularly about the other person's intent, and keep the lines of communication open.

As we respect and accept each other, and as we acknowledge the value we all bring to the table, we truly build relationships, lives, and a world that is a wonderful place to be together. It is my dream that we will live in a world where people are valued, respected, and accepted for who they are no matter what their culture, religion, country, sexual preference, financial situation, education, or gender. It is my dream to live in a world filled with unity, compassion, and joy.

I wish you well in your journey to get to know yourself and others. Embrace growth, the richness diversity brings, and a fascination for humanity and the people around you that I share. I thank you all for creating a world in which we each can live and thrive.

The PEP Personality Process and NLP

The PEP Personality Process utilizes, integrates, and adds a completely different dimension to the body of knowledge known as NLP (neurolinguistic programming), which I have studied extensively and taught for many years. NLP is a communication model that provides simple yet powerful methods for changing behaviour and producing positive results. It is an owner's manual, so to speak, for working with our human computer: the brain.

PEP Personality Processing is a complete system within itself, describing many types of personalities and behaviours, and it can be used in conjunction with NLP. It shows how we utilize the four components in the four zones, which is something totally new and different from NLP. This can add so much more depth to this already wonderful body of knowledge, and yet it is a complete stand-alone system from NLP as well.

You don't need to know anything about NLP to use this system, and if you already know about NLP, this only adds more tools to your toolbox.

About the Author

Nadine has had a life journey of inquisitiveness and an educational journey of diversity. She developed people skills because her family moved a lot and she had to figure out how to fit in to new environments on a regular basis. She has a thirst for knowledge and learning, with many interests, including people, the mind, spirituality, meditation, travelling, healthy food, science, and saving our environment.

One of the interesting things about Nadine is that she started taking workshops at the young age of 15 and did her first meditation course at the age of 16. Her thirst for learning and understanding what makes people tick, along with a desire to help others, was a powerful driver in her life.

Since her father was an entrepreneur, it is no surprise that she opened her first business at just 19, which was a sporting goods store. It was the third business in Canada to sell Windsurfers. She learned business by being totally immersed in it because, as she will tell you, as a business owner you do everything from the ground up.

She then went on to successfully manage the advertising department of a local independent newspaper, where she learned about marketing and advertising. During that time, she continued her studies, and as a side business, she gave personal growth workshops and organized Reiki retreats. This side business was where her passion was. Her heart was in assisting people to have a better quality of life.

Nadine continued her studies in counselling, worked with Mid-Island Hospice as a volunteer, and became certified as a counsellor in private practice. Wanting even more tools and skills, she studied with some of the most well-known teachers and trainers in neurolinguistic programming (NLP) and was eventually certified as a NLP trainer and master hypnotherapist herself.

She opened her first private practice in her home and then opened a wellness clinic where she did counselling and personal enrichment programs. Her partner in the clinic did iridology and nutrition, and Nadine was intrigued by that field. With her passion for learning, she then went to California, trained with Dr Bernard Jensen, and got her certification as an iridologist and nutritionist to add to her business repertoire.

In 1989, she moved her private practice to Victoria, British Columbia, where her self-esteem programs for both men and women were very well received and her practice flourished. Her philosophy has always been that her job was to work herself out of a job.

In 1994, wanting to share her knowledge, she opened a private post-secondary training institution where she has taught NLP, hypnosis, TimeLine therapy and counselling skills to her students.

Today, Nadine is an author, speaker, counsellor, coach, facilitator, and trainer. She has raised two wonderful daughters and lives with her husband, Heinz, in Victoria. She says her next learning curve will be creating online courses and writing her next book.

CPSIA information can be obtained
at www.ICGtesting.com
Printed in the USA
FFHW020027250119
50276297-55326FF